SACRAMENTO PUBLIC LIBRARY
828 "I" STREET
SACRAMENTO, CA 95814

1/2010

D0955969

The Gift of the Magi

O. Henry's
The Gift of the Magi

by
Joel Priddy

itbooks

AN IMPRINT OF HARPERCOLLINS PUBLISHERS

This book is a work of fiction. The characters, incidents, and dialogue are drawn from the author's imagination and are not to be construed as real. Any resemblance to actual events or persons, living or dead, is entirely coincidental.

THE GIFT OF THE MAGI. Copyright © 2009 by Joel Priddy. All rights reserved. Printed in China. No part of this book may be used or reproduced in any manner whatsoever without written permission except in the case of brief quotations embodied in critical articles and reviews. For information address HarperCollins Publishers, 10 East 53rd Street, New York, NY 10022.

HarperCollins books may be purchased for educational, business, or sales promotional use. For information please write: Special Markets Department, HarperCollins Publishers, 10 East 53rd Street, New York, NY 10022.

FIRST EDITION

ISBN 978-0-06-178239-8

09 10 11 12 13   10 9 8 7 6 5 4 3 2 1

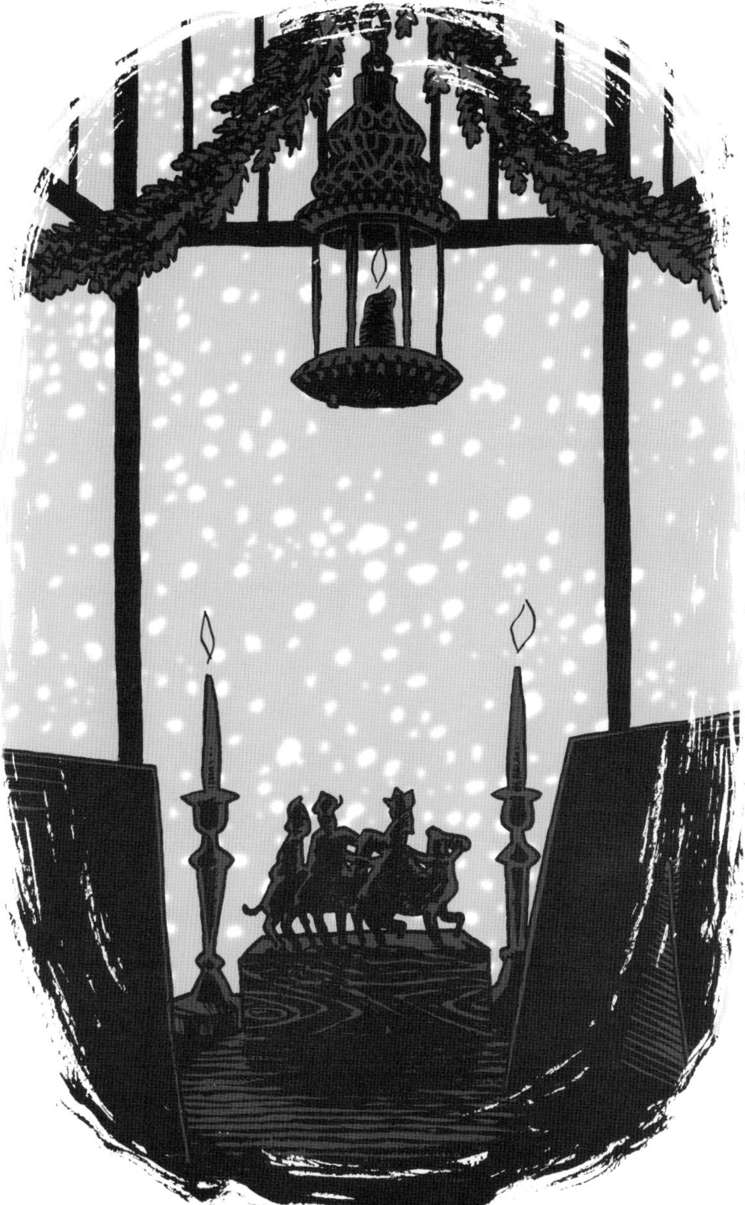

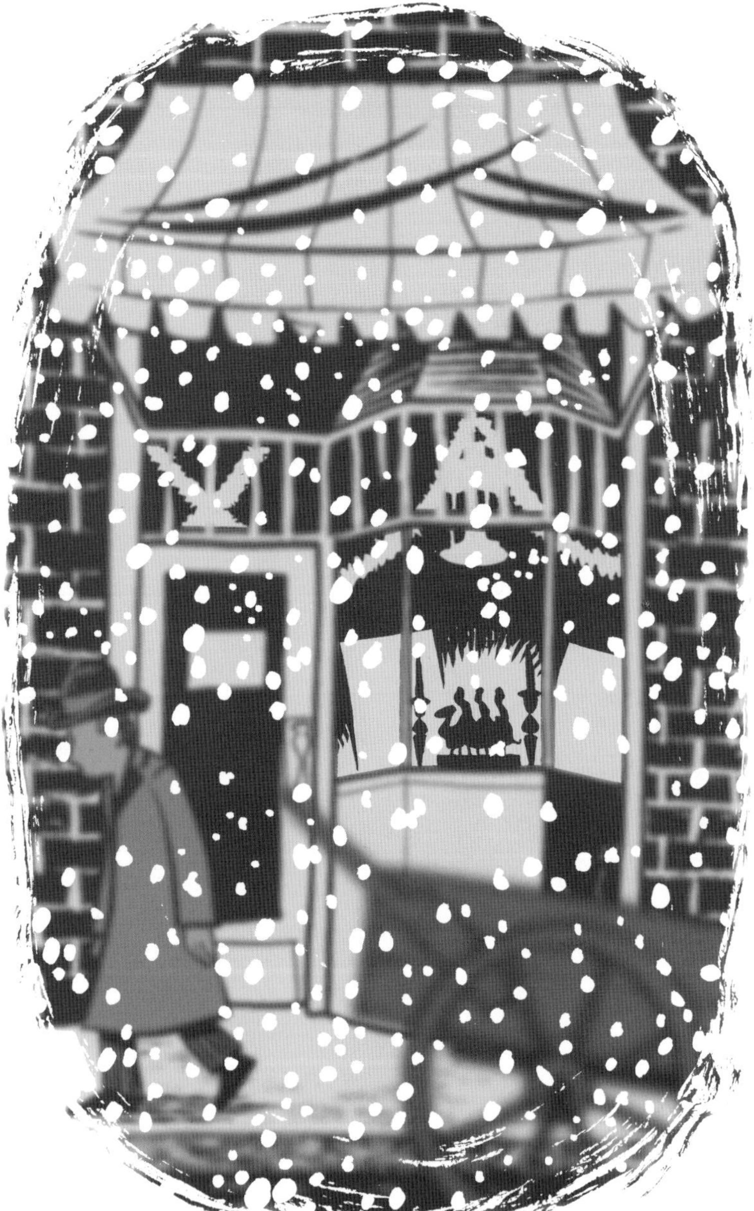

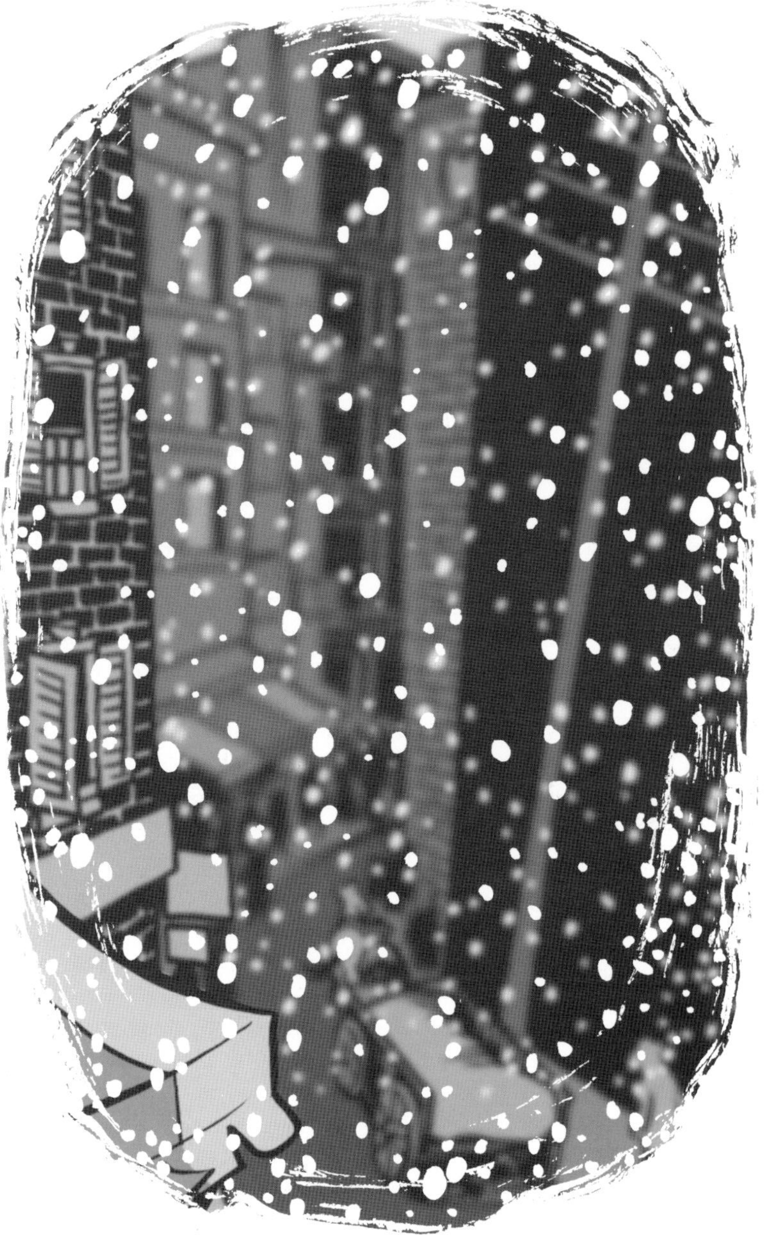

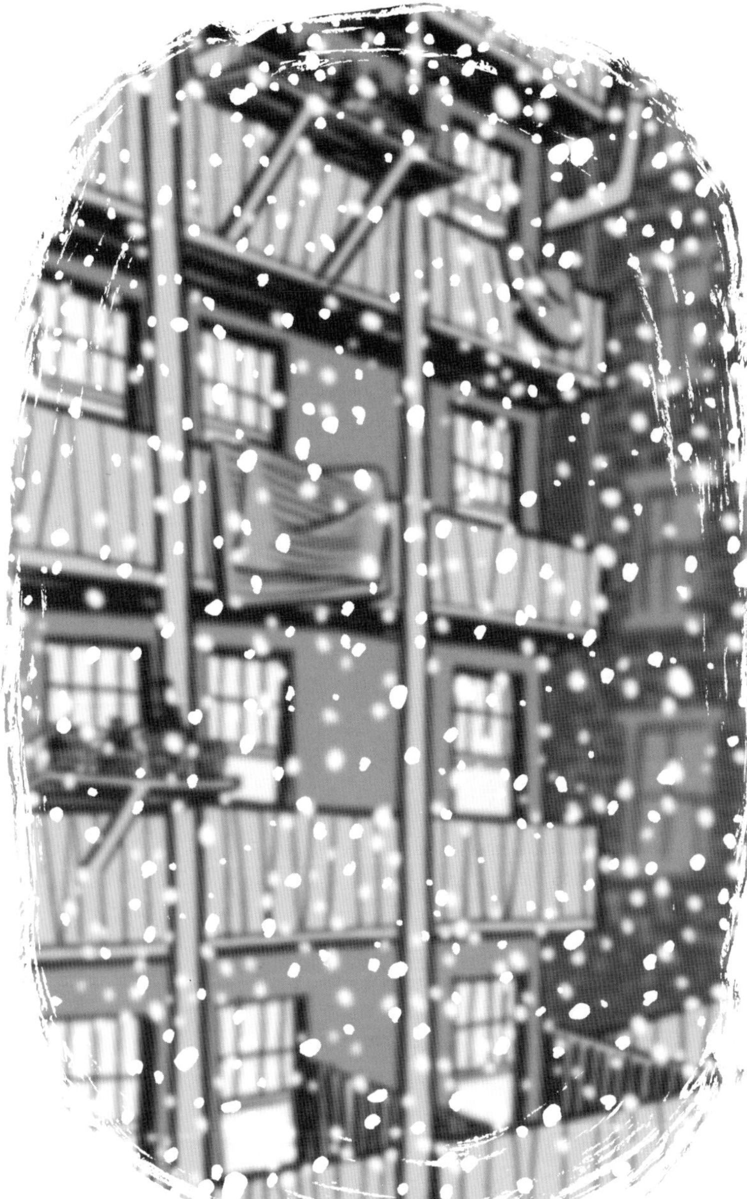

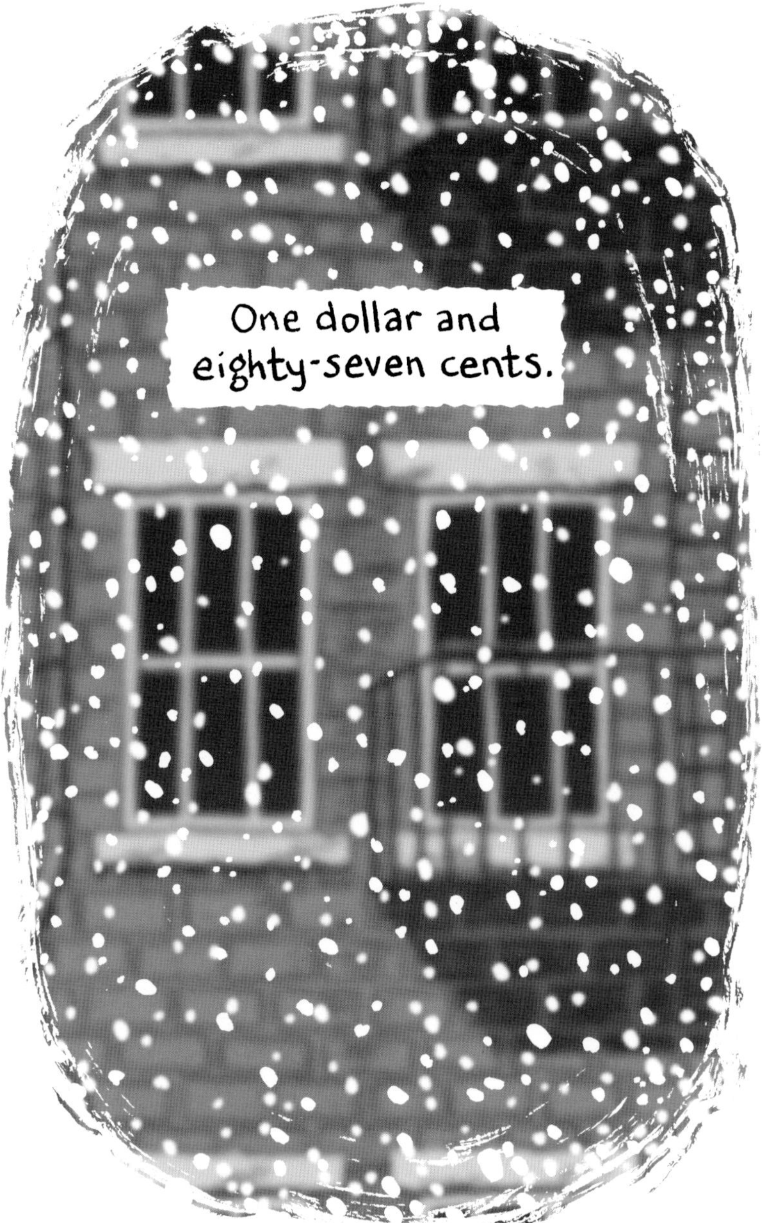
One dollar and
eighty-seven cents.

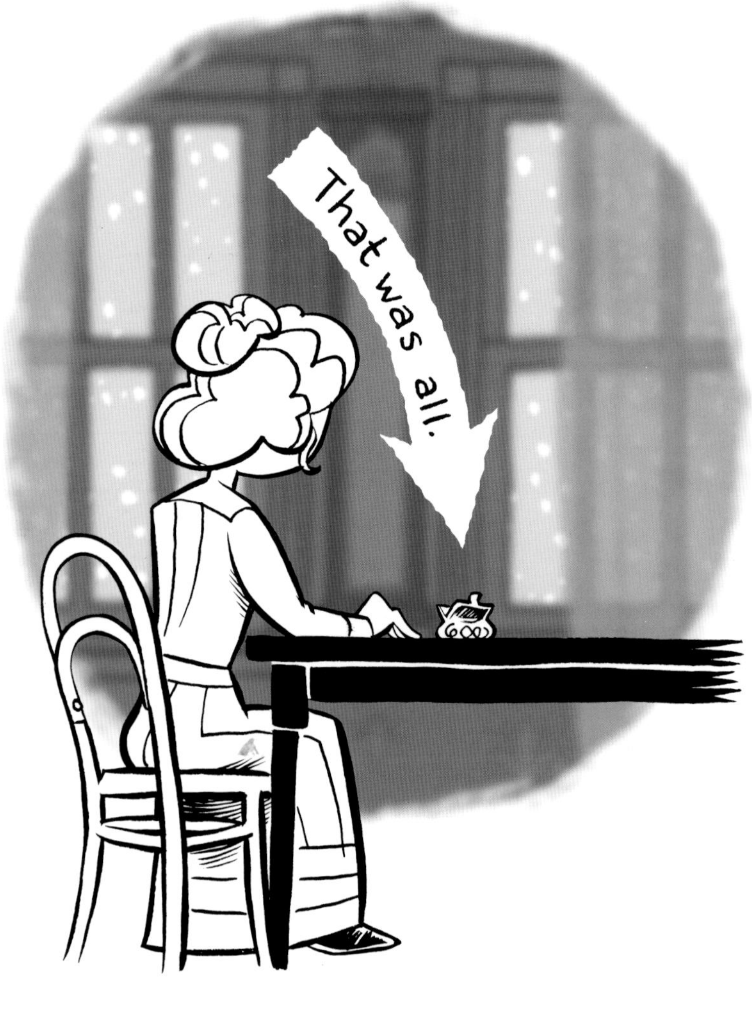
That was all.

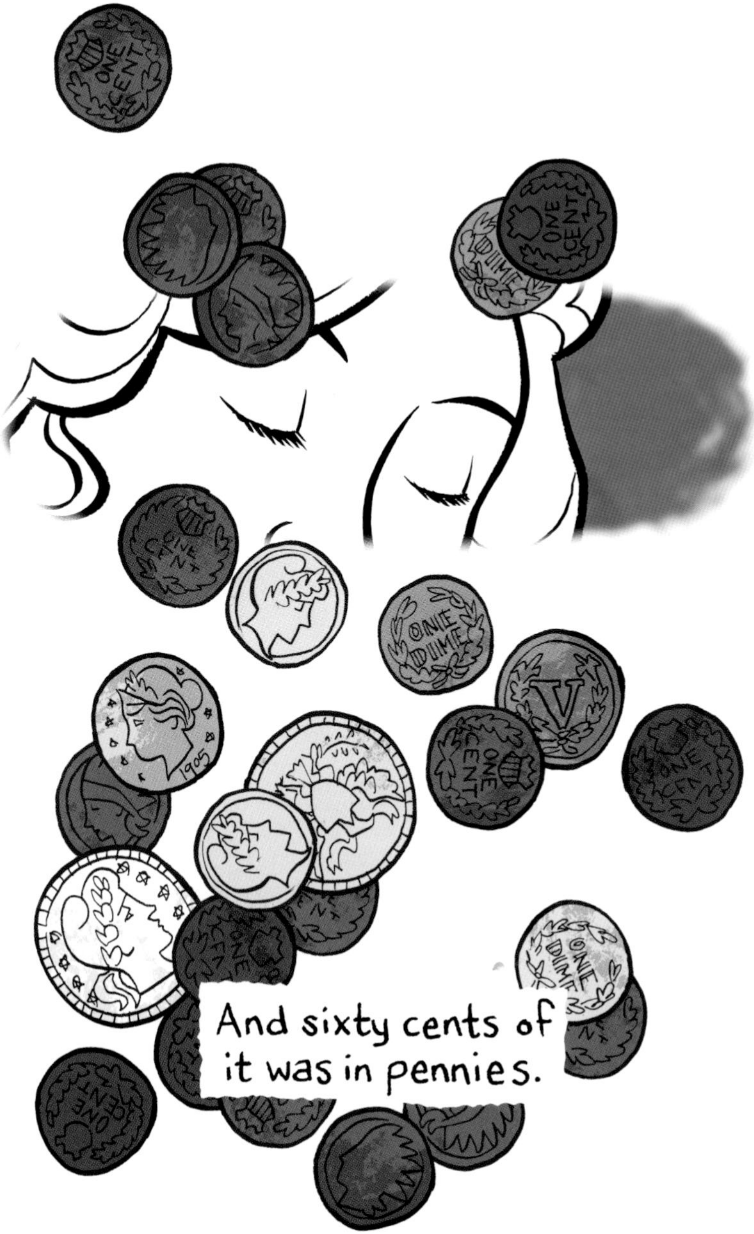
And sixty cents of it was in pennies.

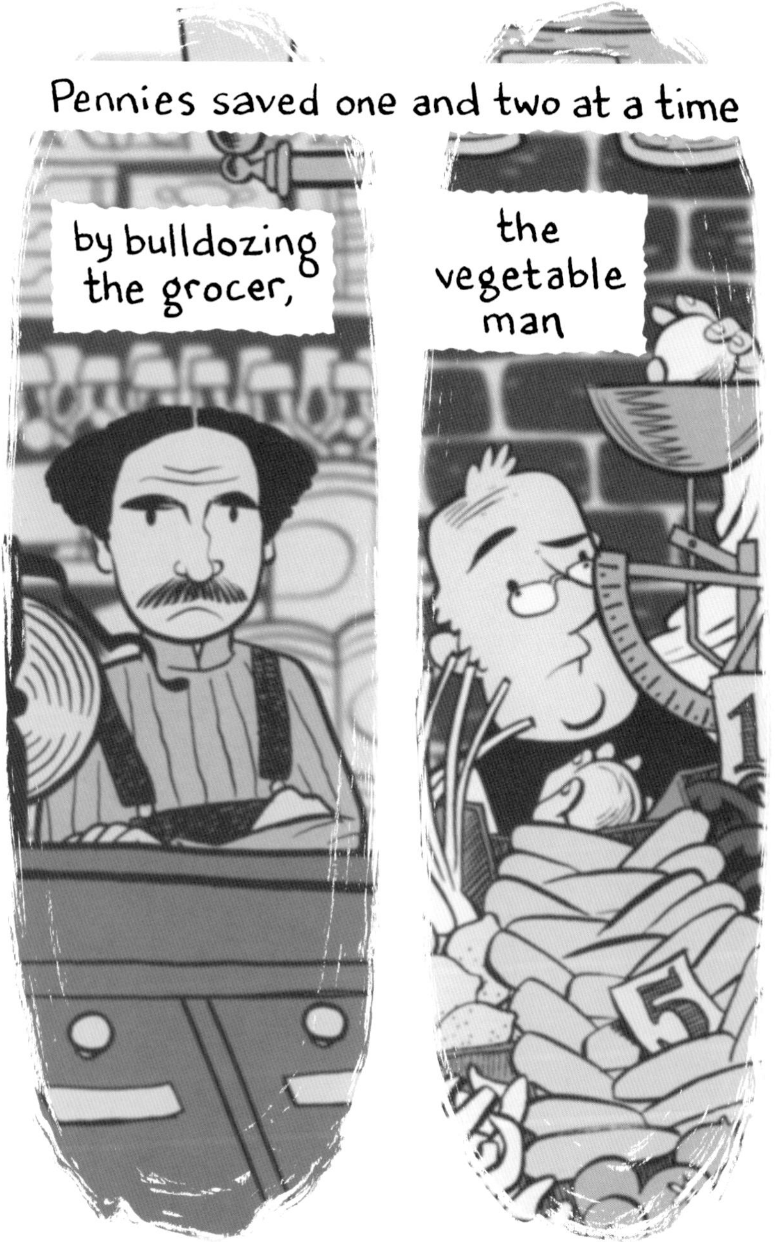
Pennies saved one and two at a time
by bulldozing the grocer,
the vegetable man

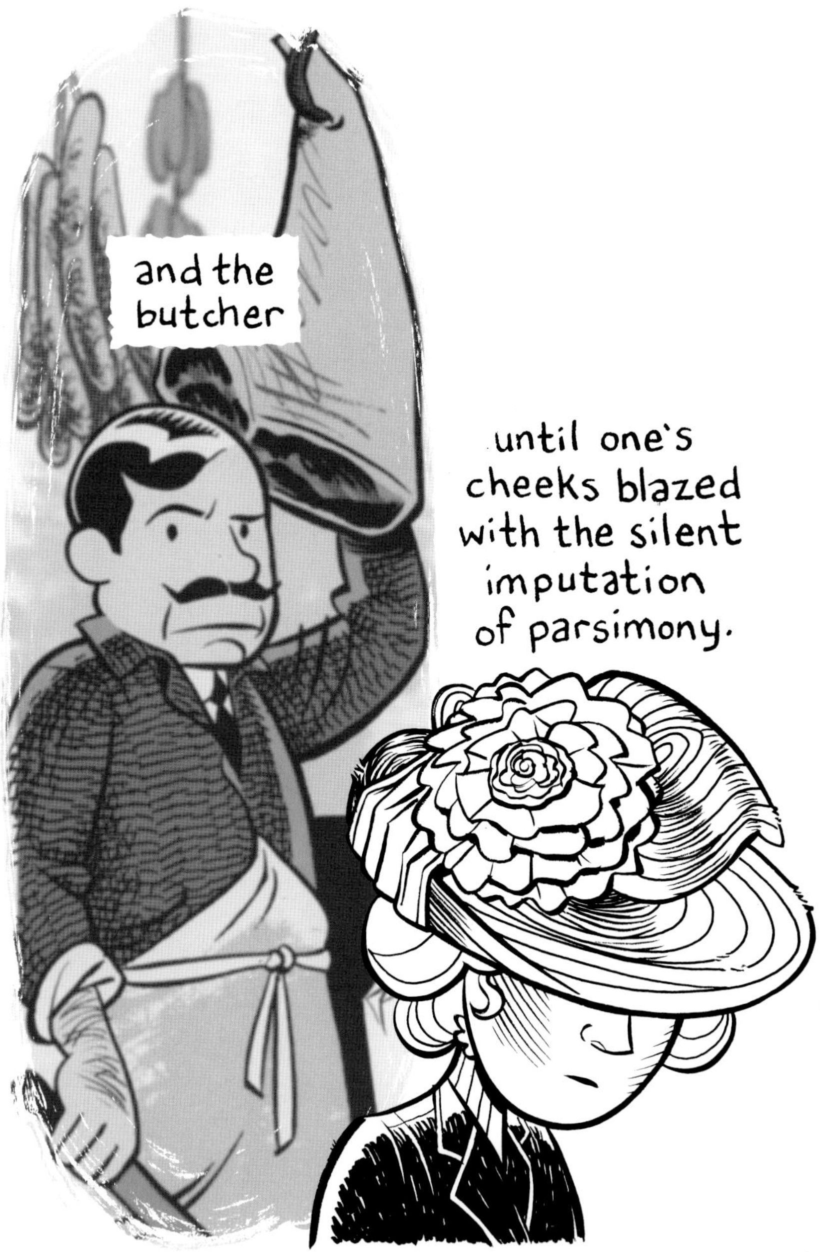
and the butcher
until one's cheeks blazed with the silent imputation of parsimony.

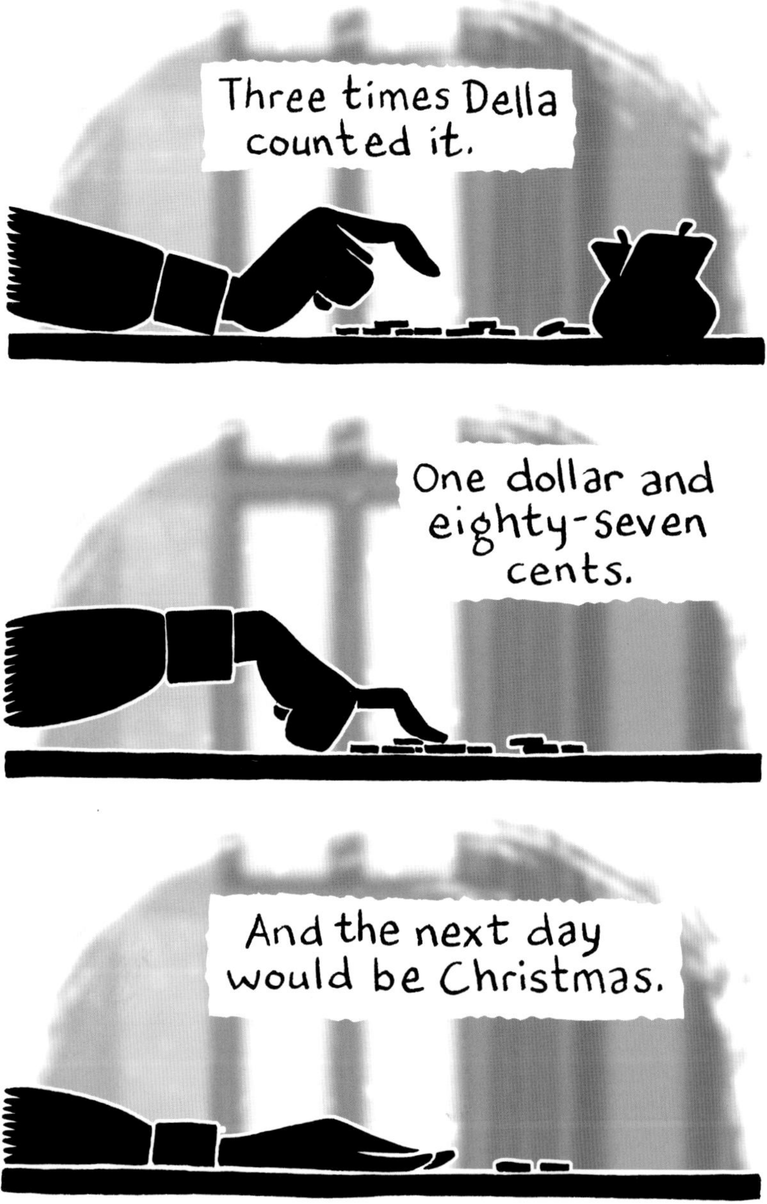
Three times Della counted it.
One dollar and eighty-seven cents.
And the next day would be Christmas.

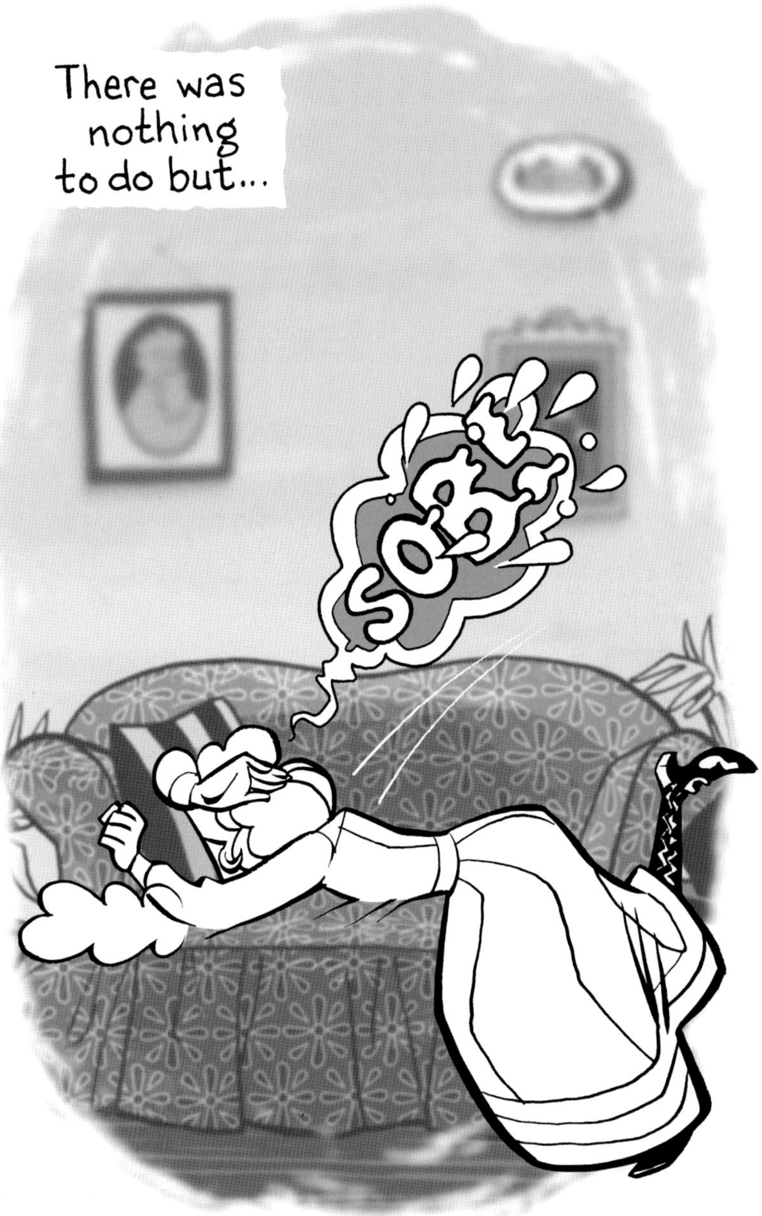
There was nothing to do but...
SOB!

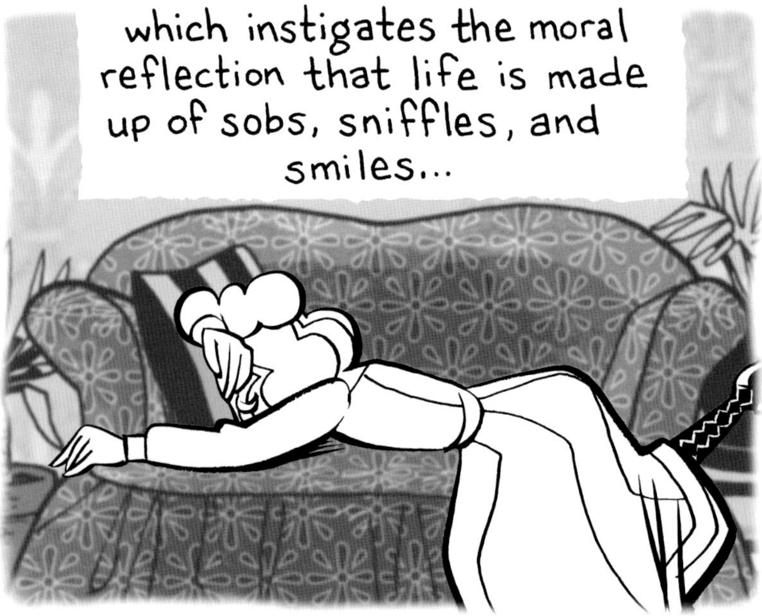
which instigates the moral reflection that life is made up of sobs, sniffles, and smiles...

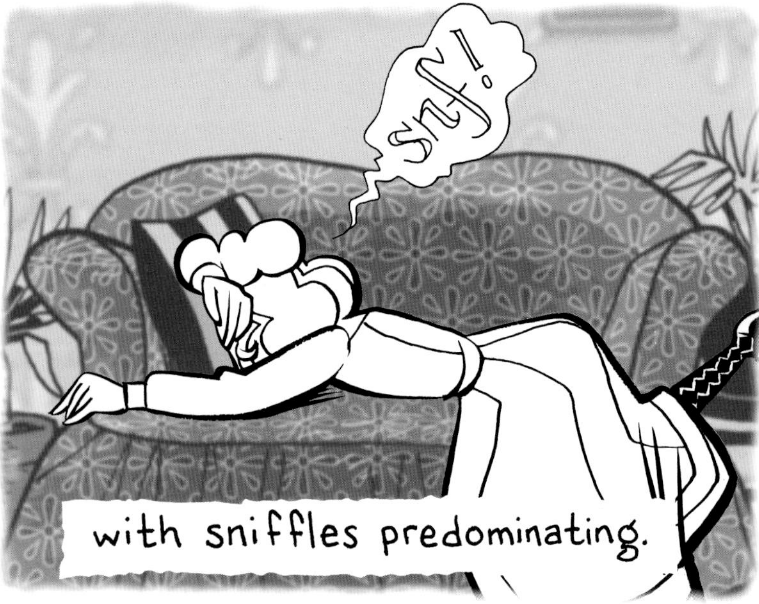
snf!
with sniffles predominating.

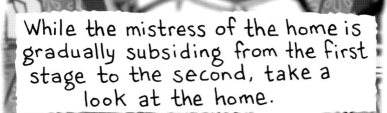

While the mistress of the home is gradually subsiding from the first stage to the second, take a look at the home.

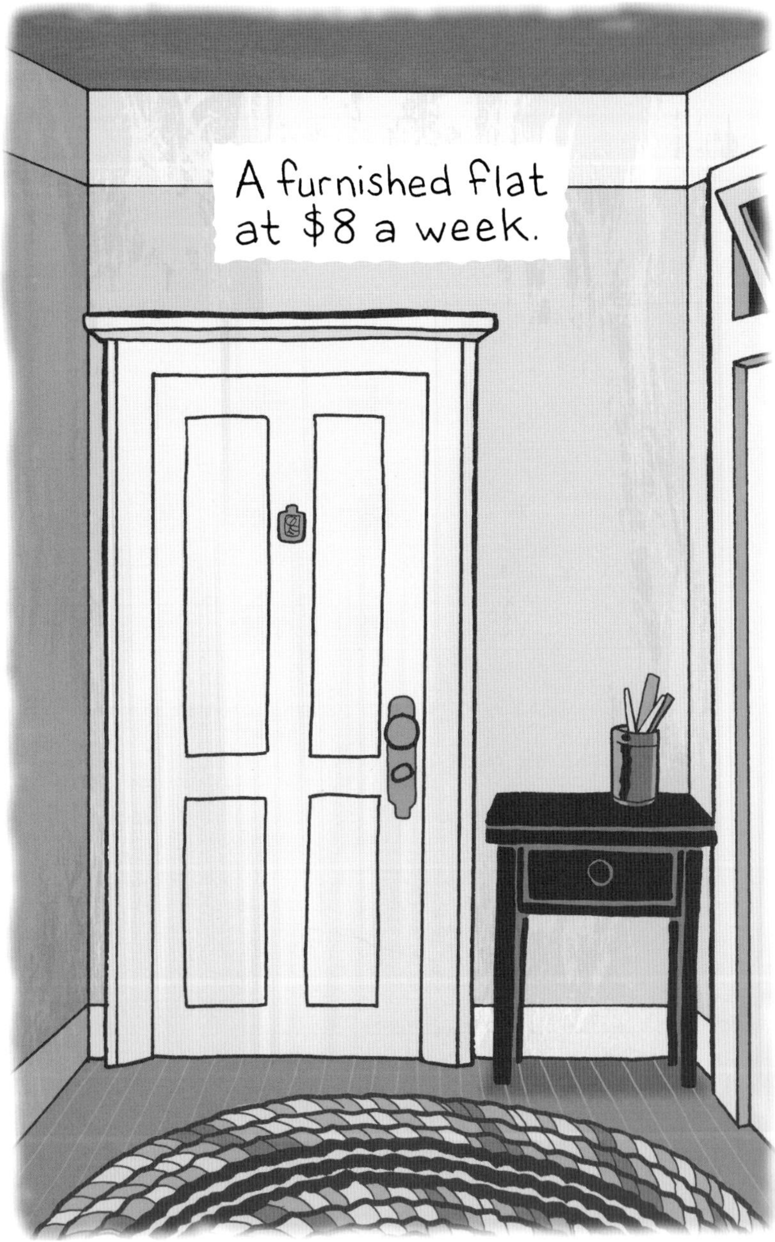
A furnished flat at $8 a week.

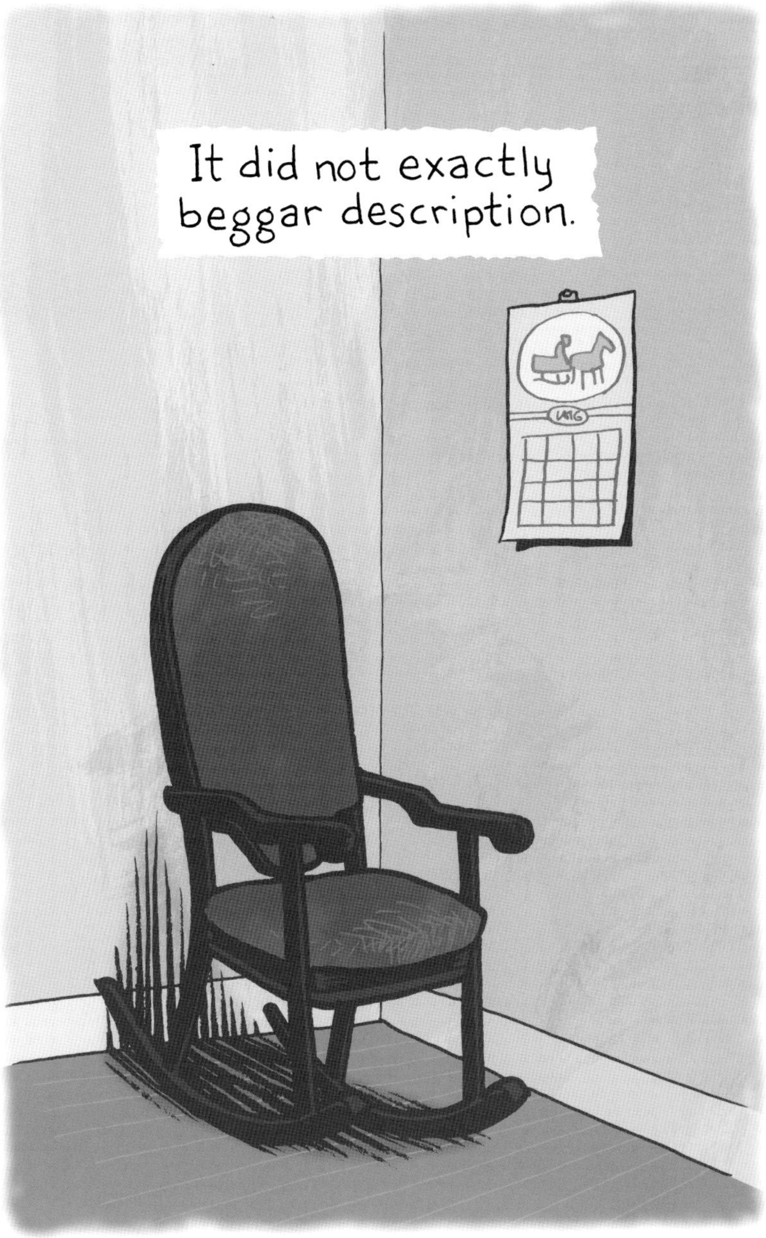
It did not exactly beggar description.

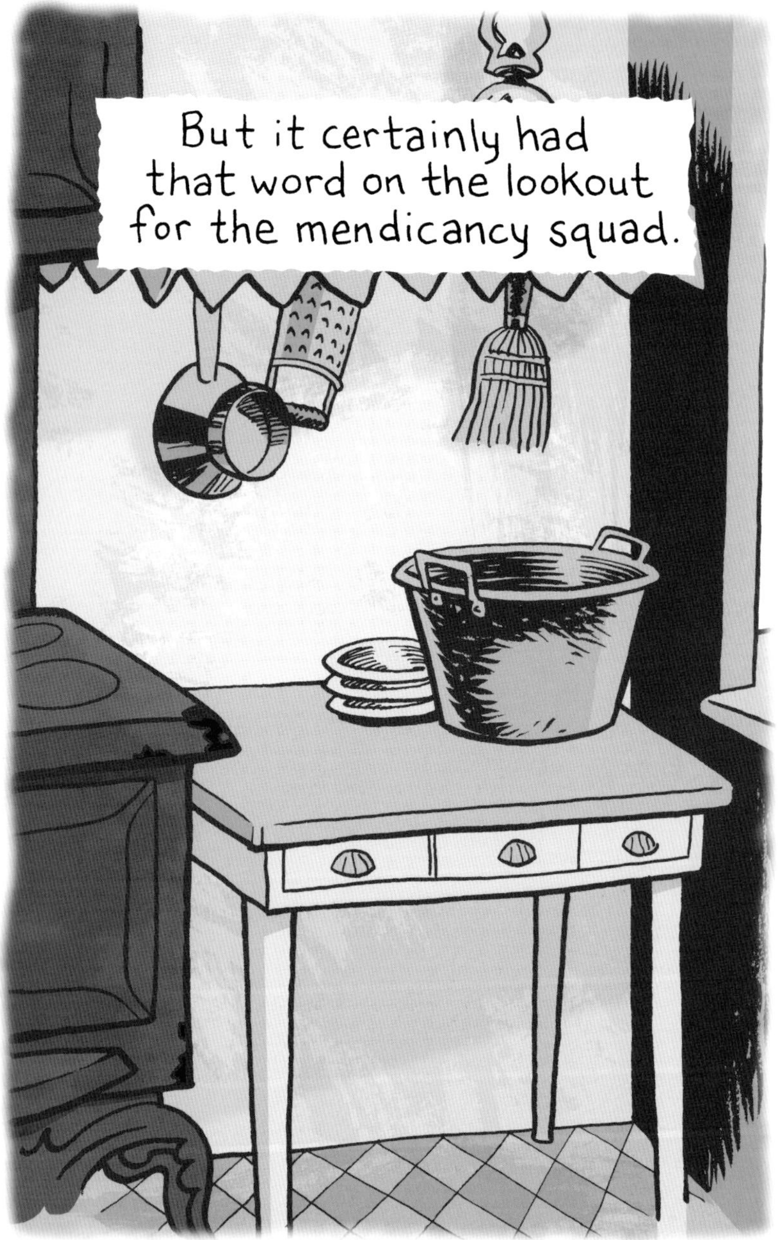
But it certainly had that word on the lookout for the mendicancy squad.

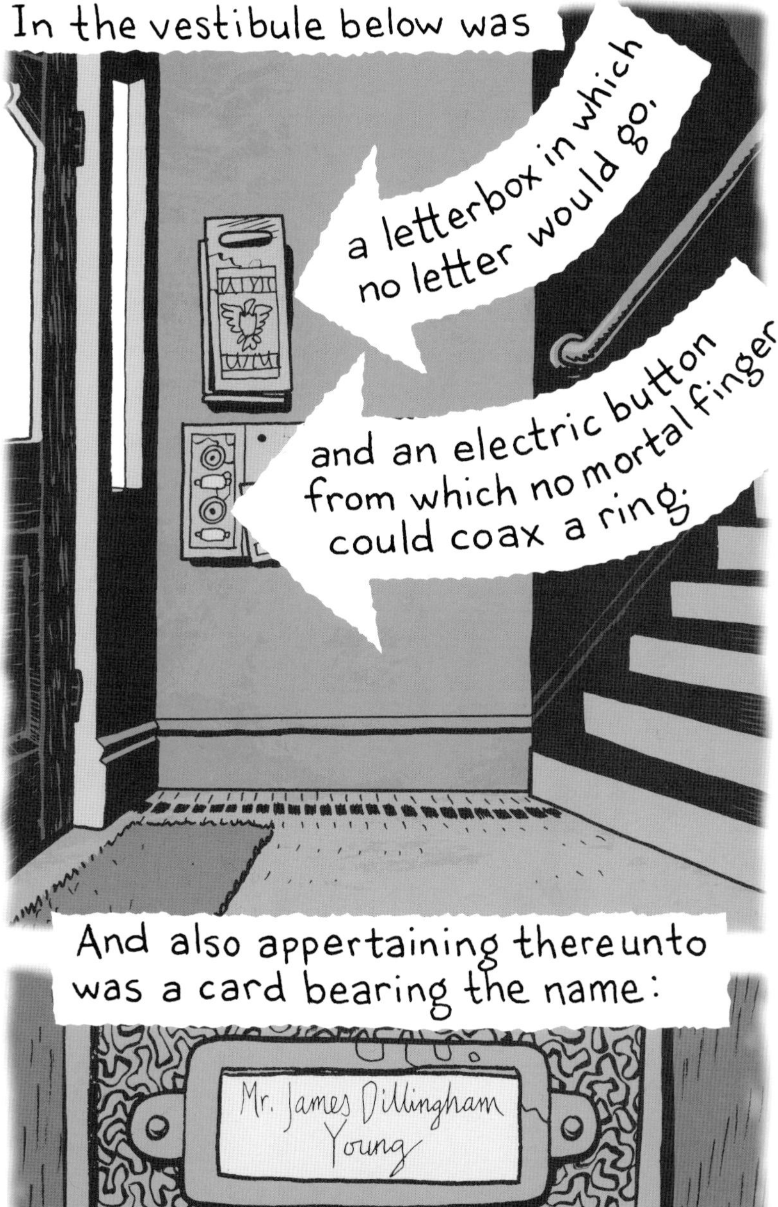
In the vestibule below was
a letterbox in which no letter would go,
and an electric button from which no mortal finger could coax a ring.
And also appertaining thereunto was a card bearing the name:
Mr. James Dillingham Young

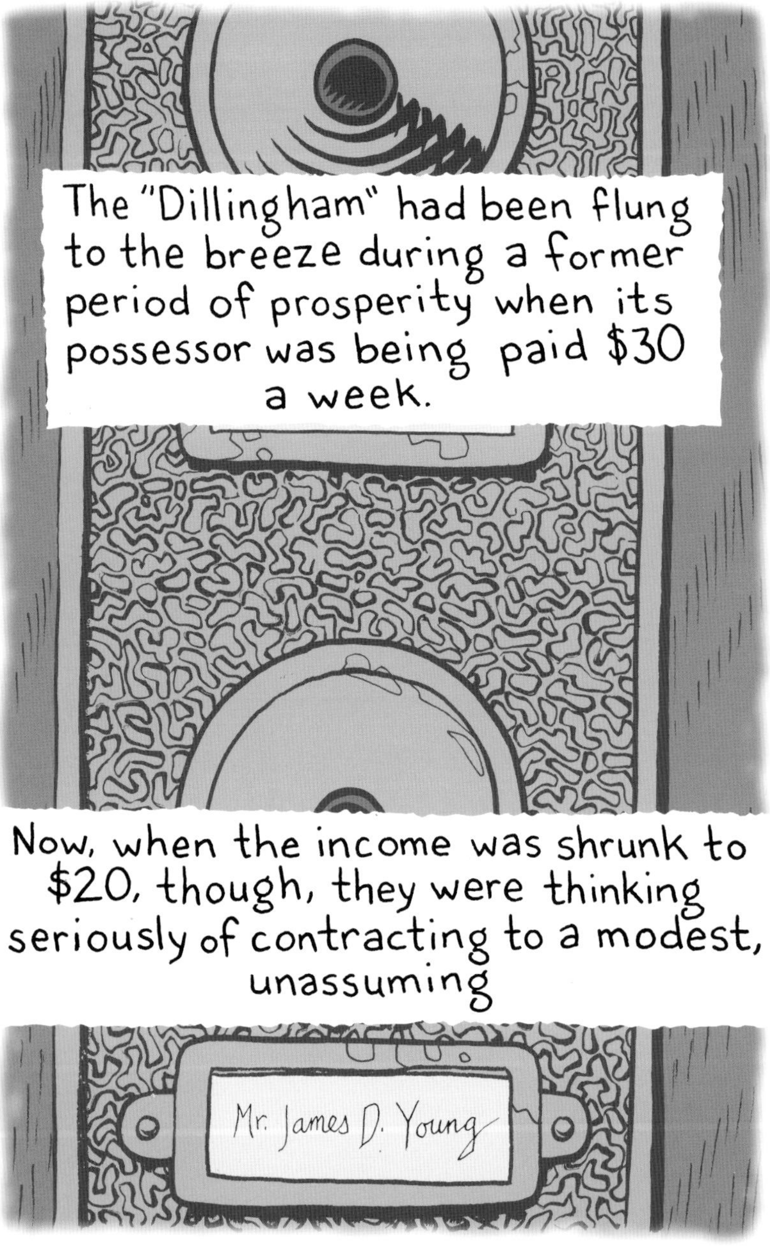
The "Dillingham" had been flung to the breeze during a former period of prosperity when its possessor was being paid $30 a week.
Now, when the income was shrunk to $20, though, they were thinking seriously of contracting to a modest, unassuming
Mr. James D. Young

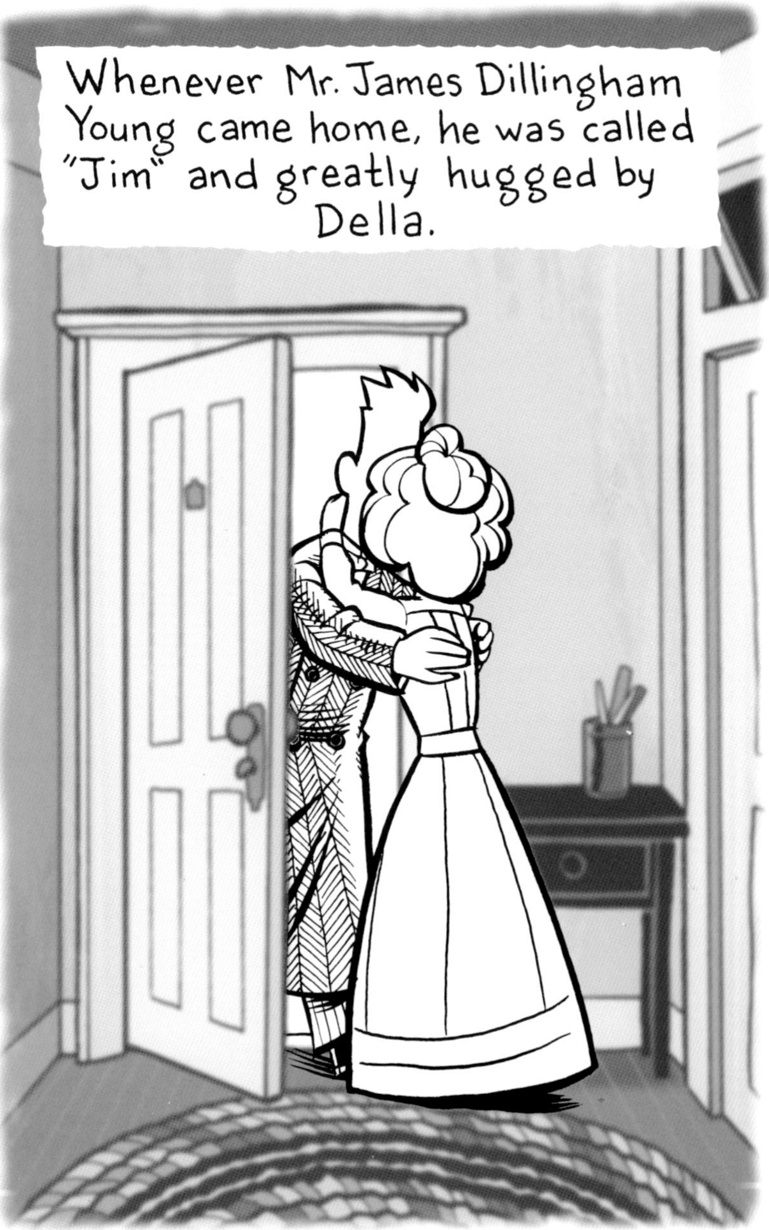
Whenever Mr. James Dillingham Young came home, he was called "Jim" and greatly hugged by Della.

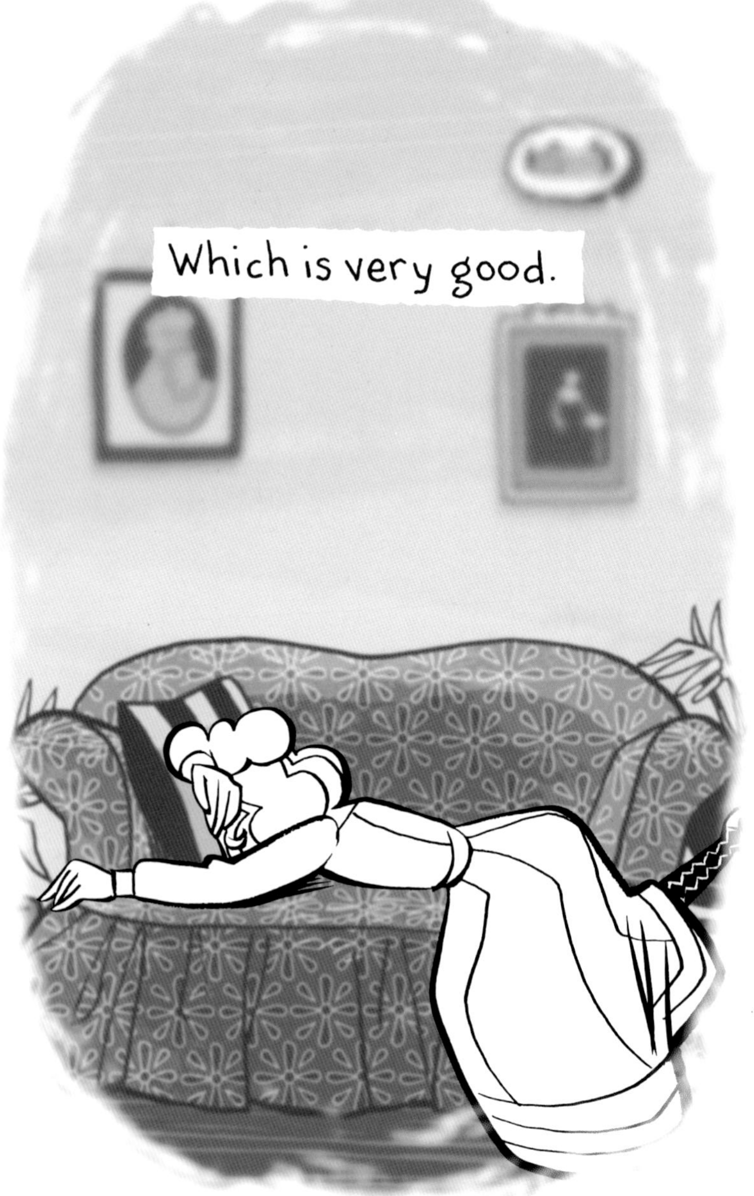
Which is very good.

Tomorrow would be Christmas Day, and she had only $1.87 with which to buy Jim a present.

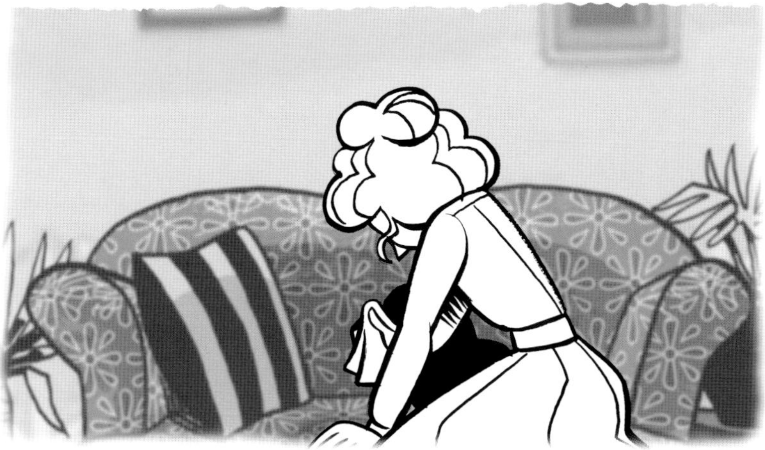

She had been saving every penny for months, with this result.

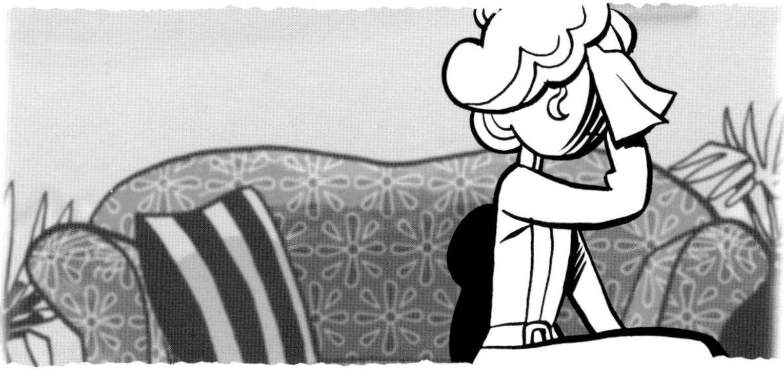

Twenty dollars a week doesn't go far.

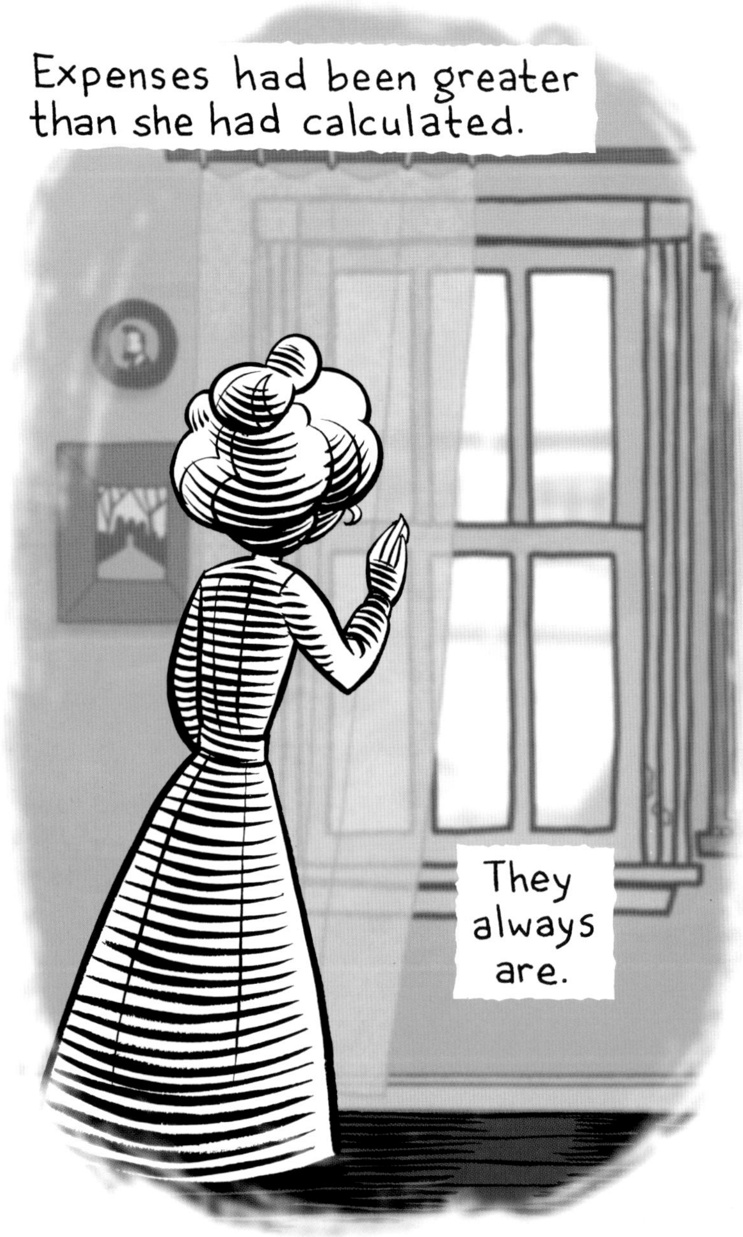
Expenses had been greater than she had calculated.
They always are.

Only $1.87 to buy a present for Jim, ***her*** Jim. Many a happy hour she had spent planning for something nice for him.

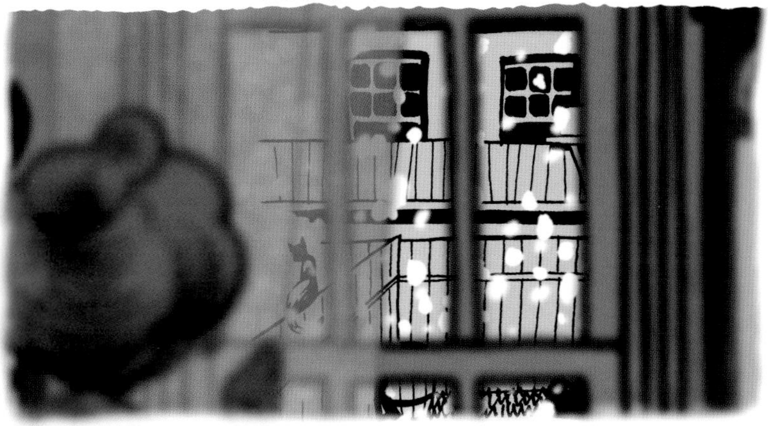

Something fine and rare and sterling— something just a little bit near to being worthy of being owned by Jim.

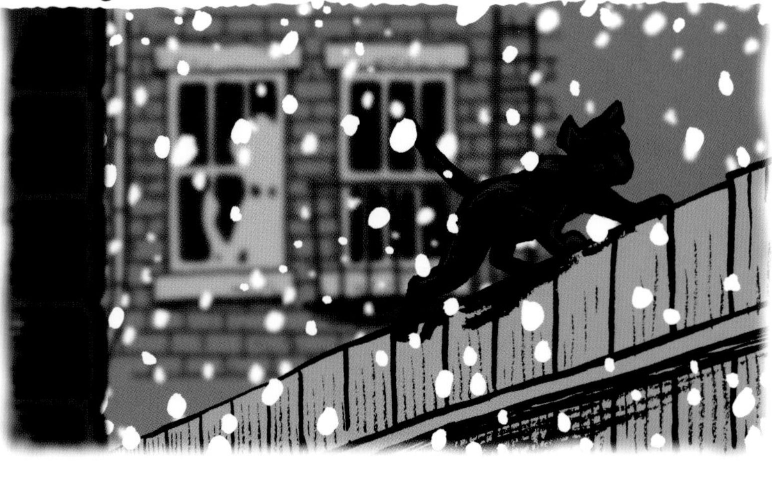

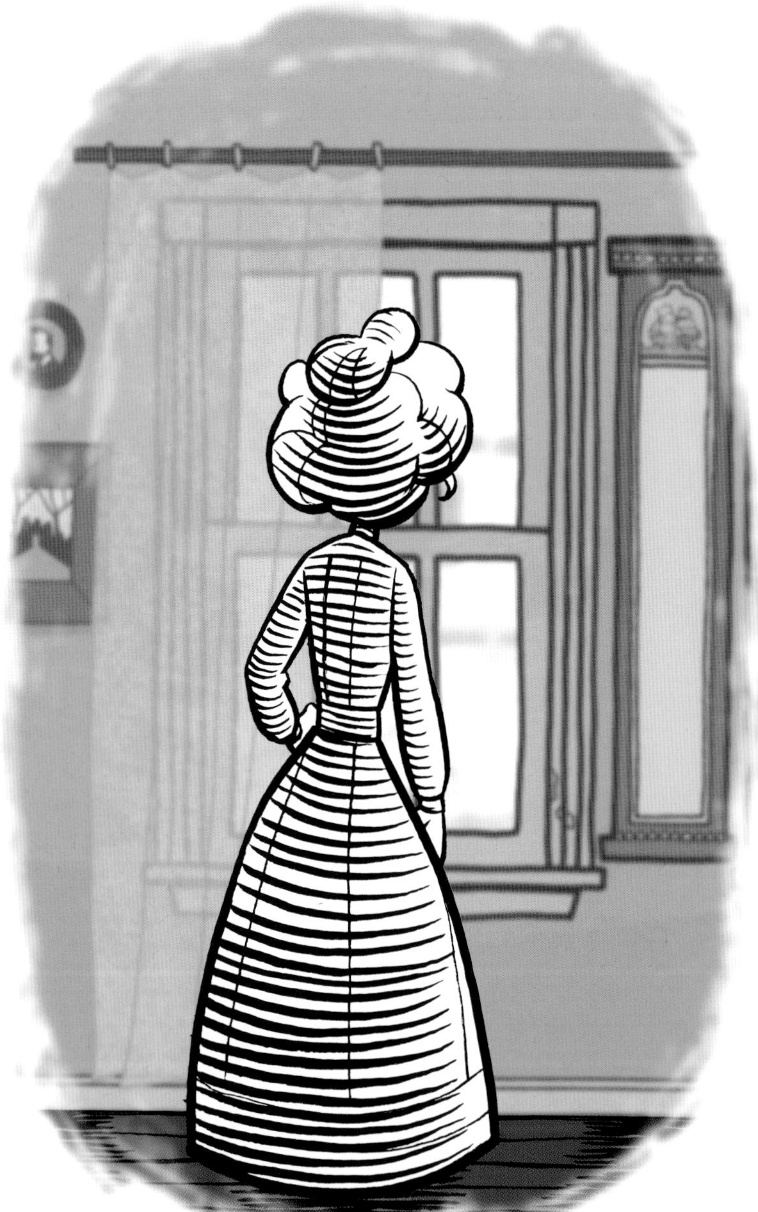

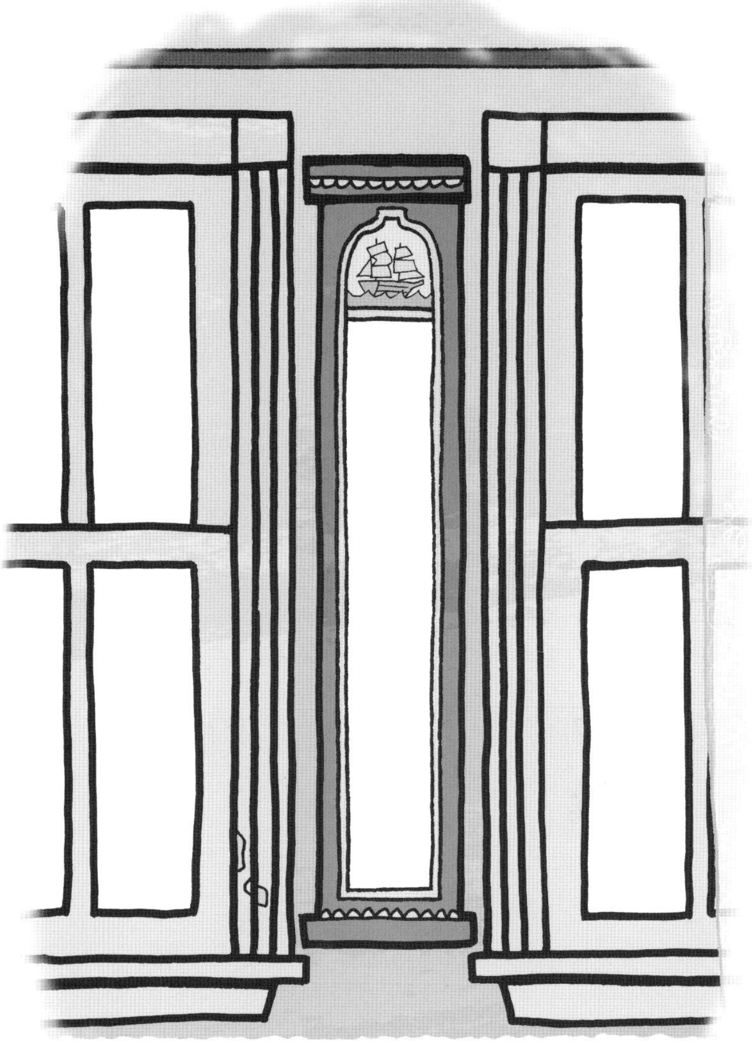

Perhaps you have seen a pier glass in an $8 flat.

A very
thin

and very
agile
person

may

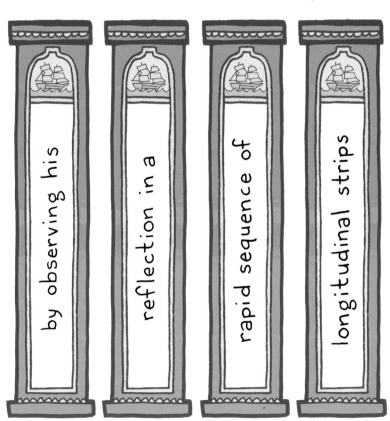

by observing his

reflection in a

rapid sequence of

longitudinal strips

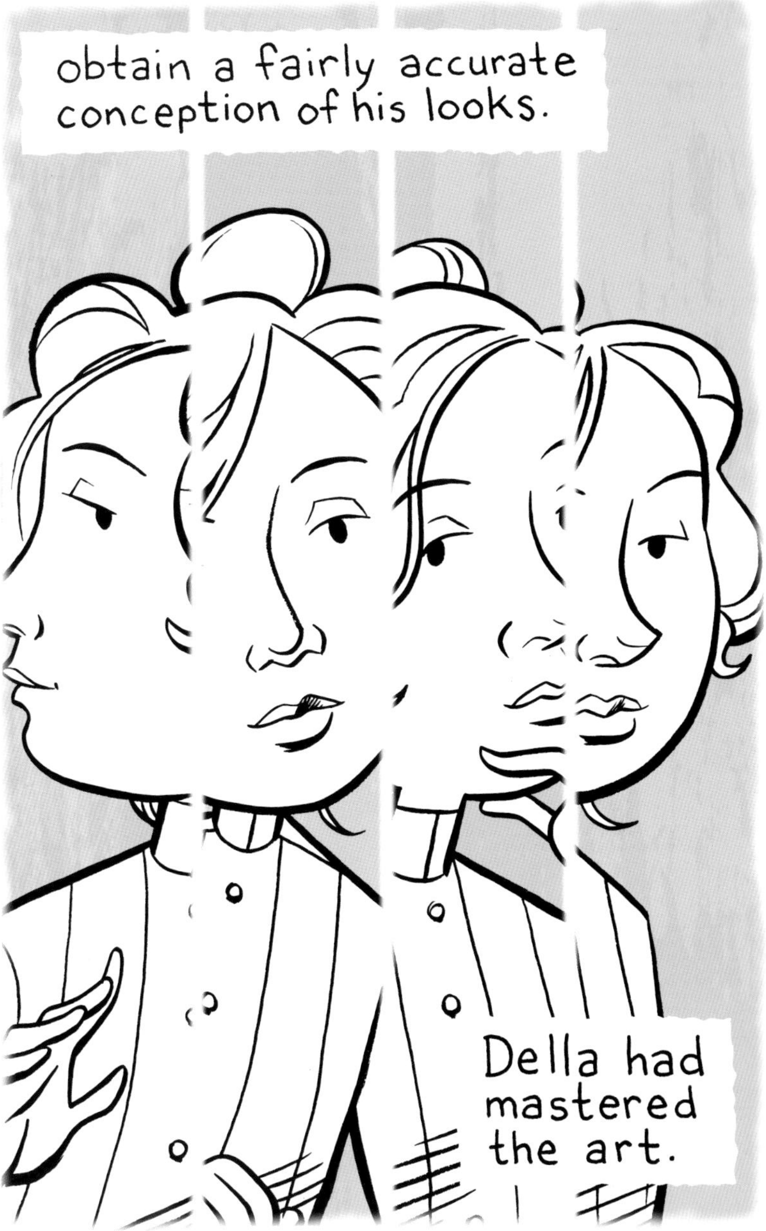
obtain a fairly accurate conception of his looks.
Della had mastered the art.

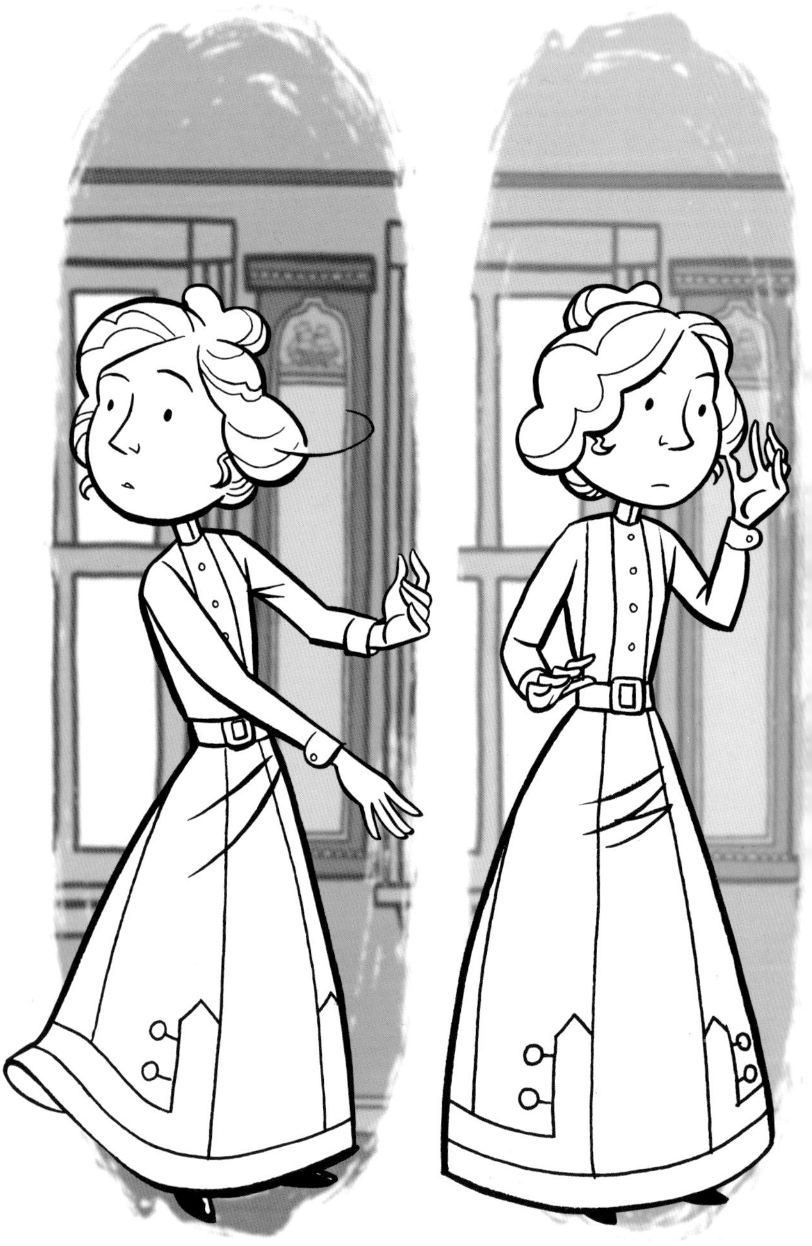

Now, there were two possessions of the James Dillingham Youngs in which they took mighty pride.

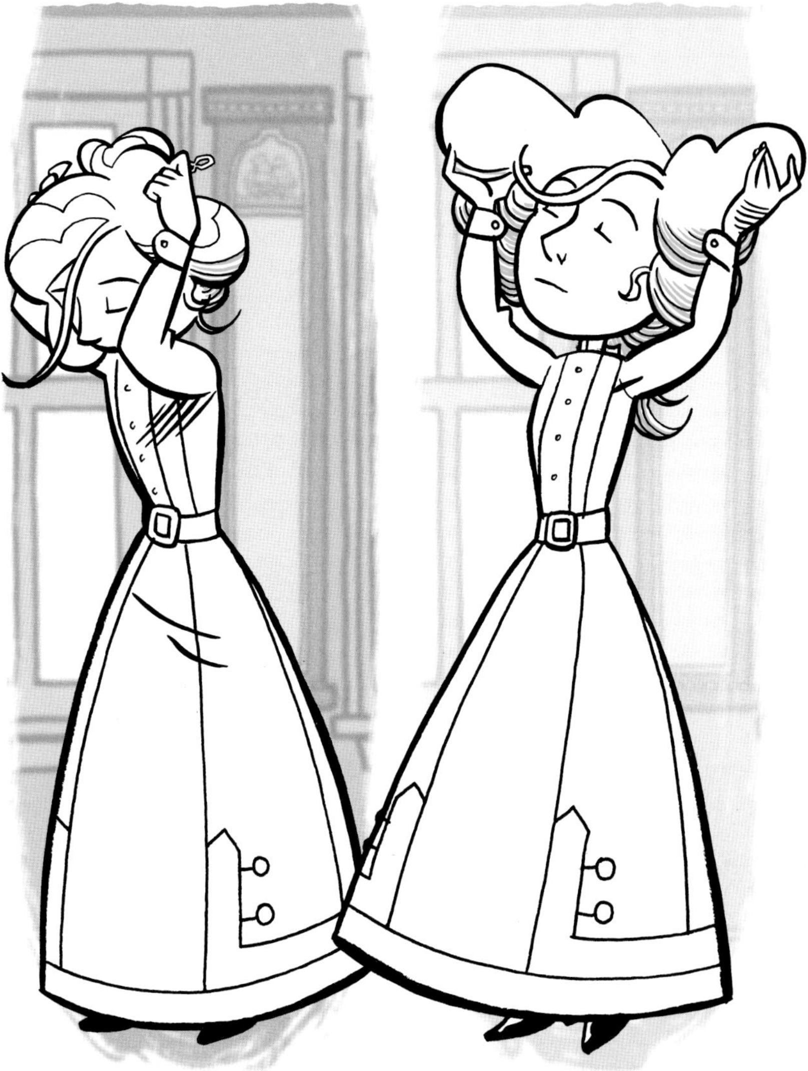

One was

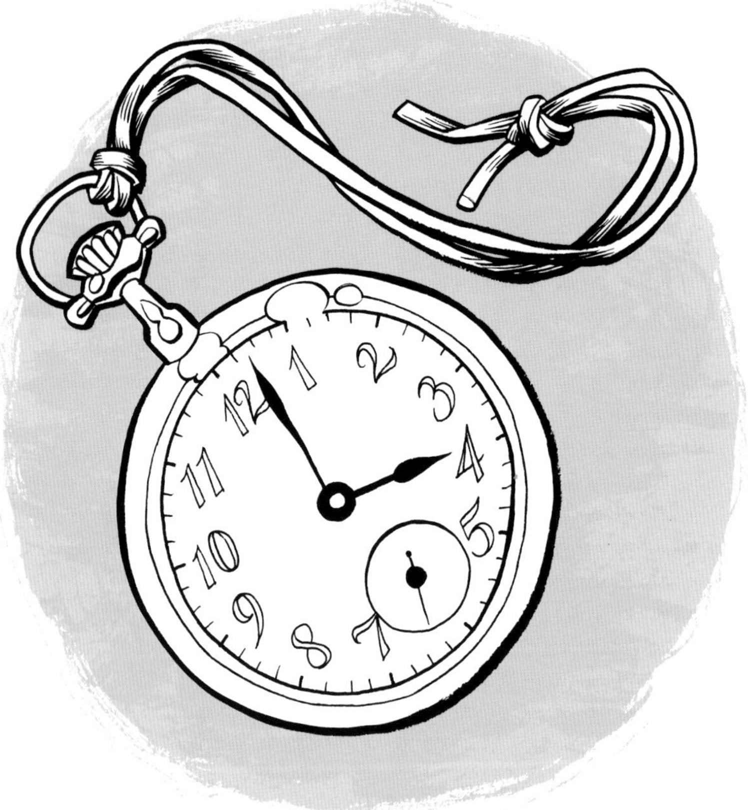

Jim's gold watch

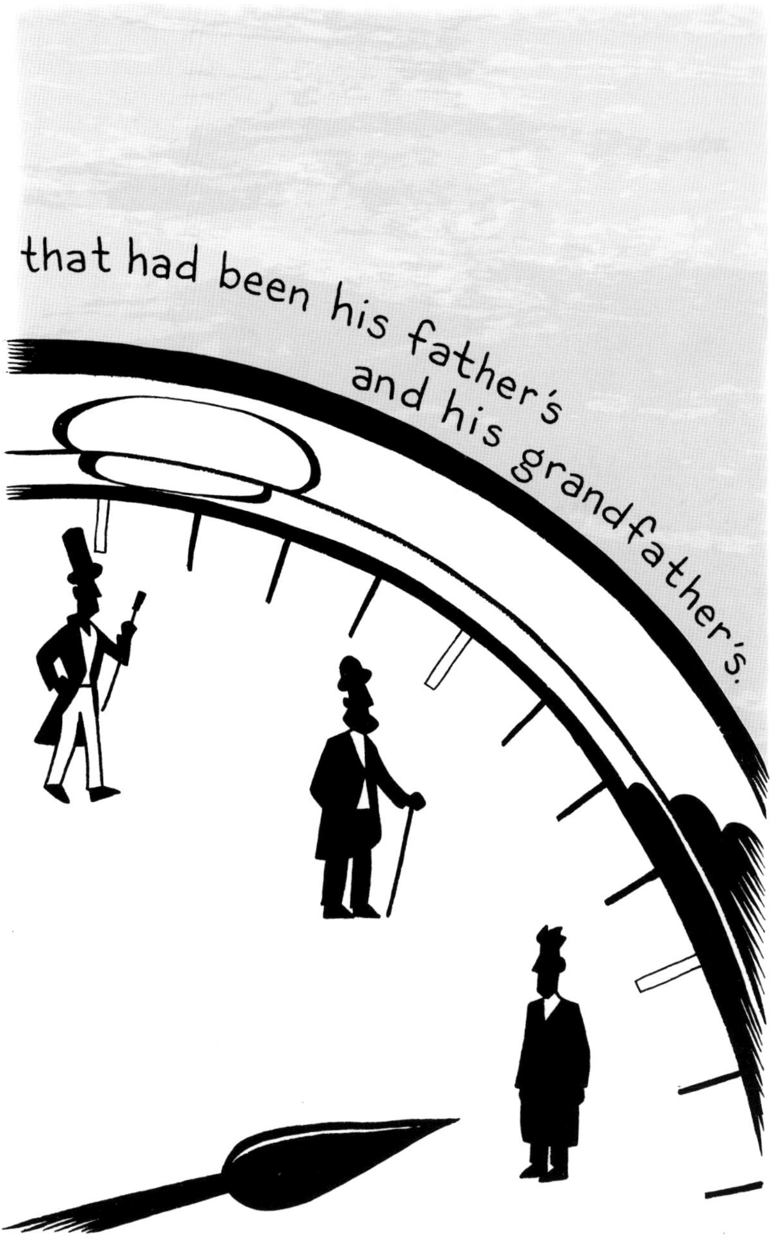
that had been his father's
and his grandfather's.

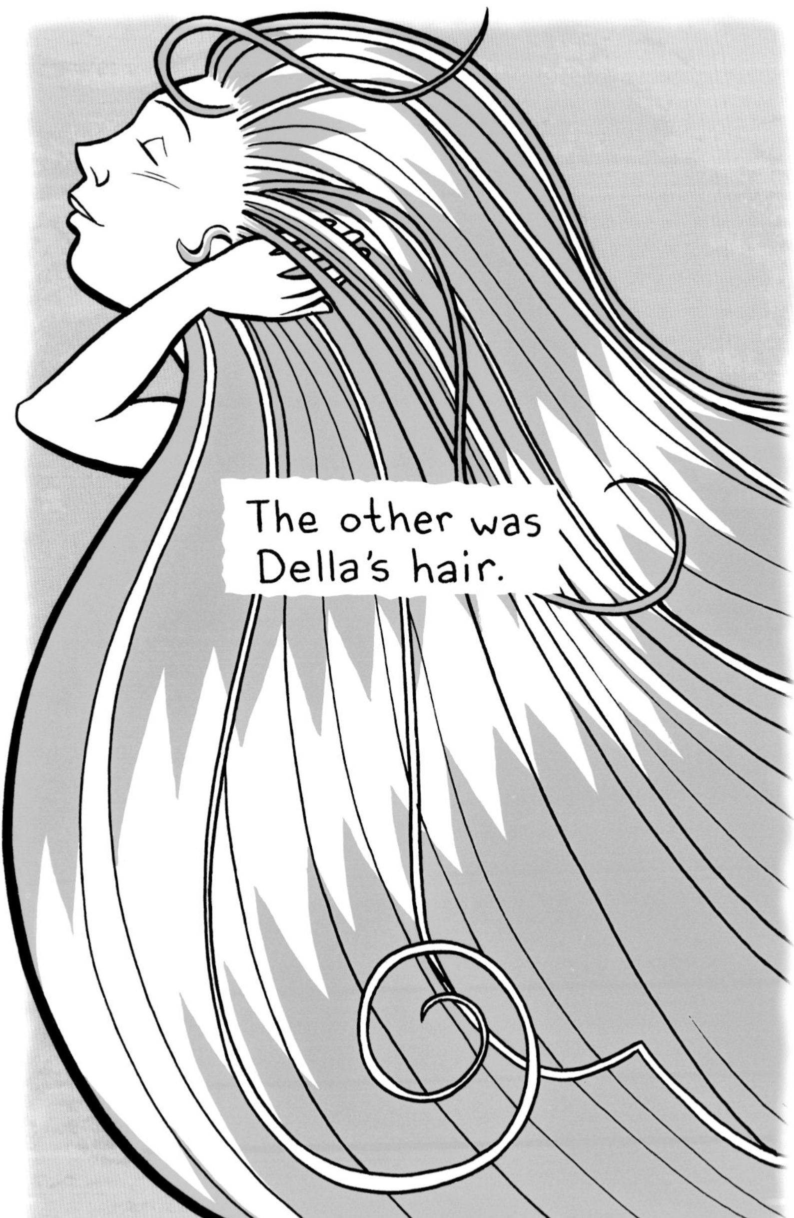
The other was Della's hair.

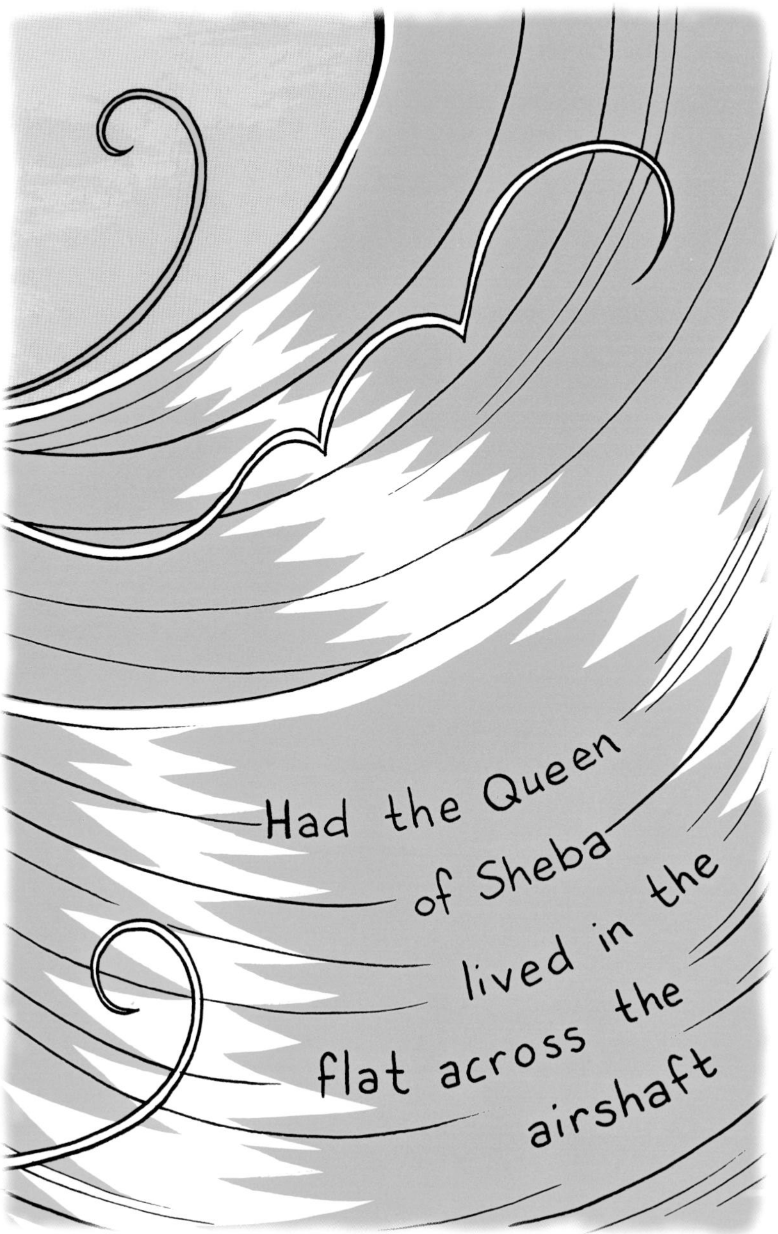
Had the Queen
of Sheba
lived in the
flat across the
airshaft

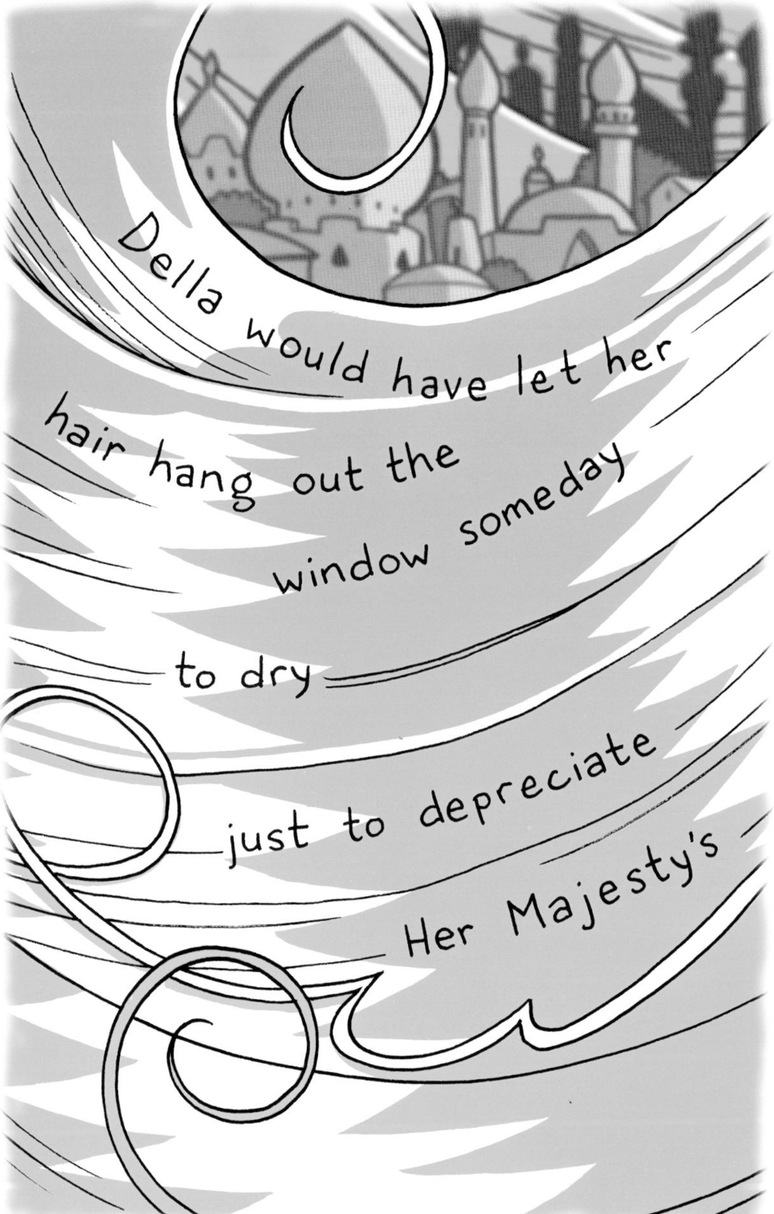
Della would have let her
hair hang out the
window someday
to dry
just to depreciate
Her Majesty's

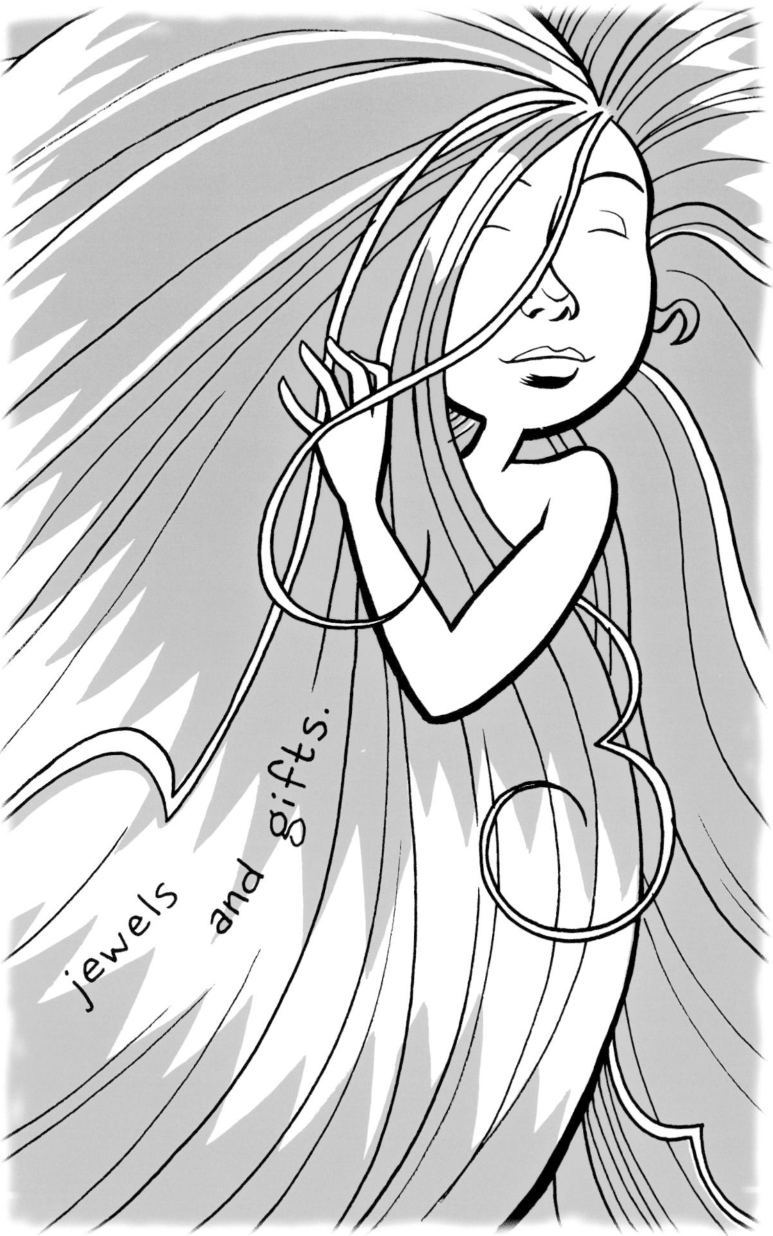
jewels and gifts.

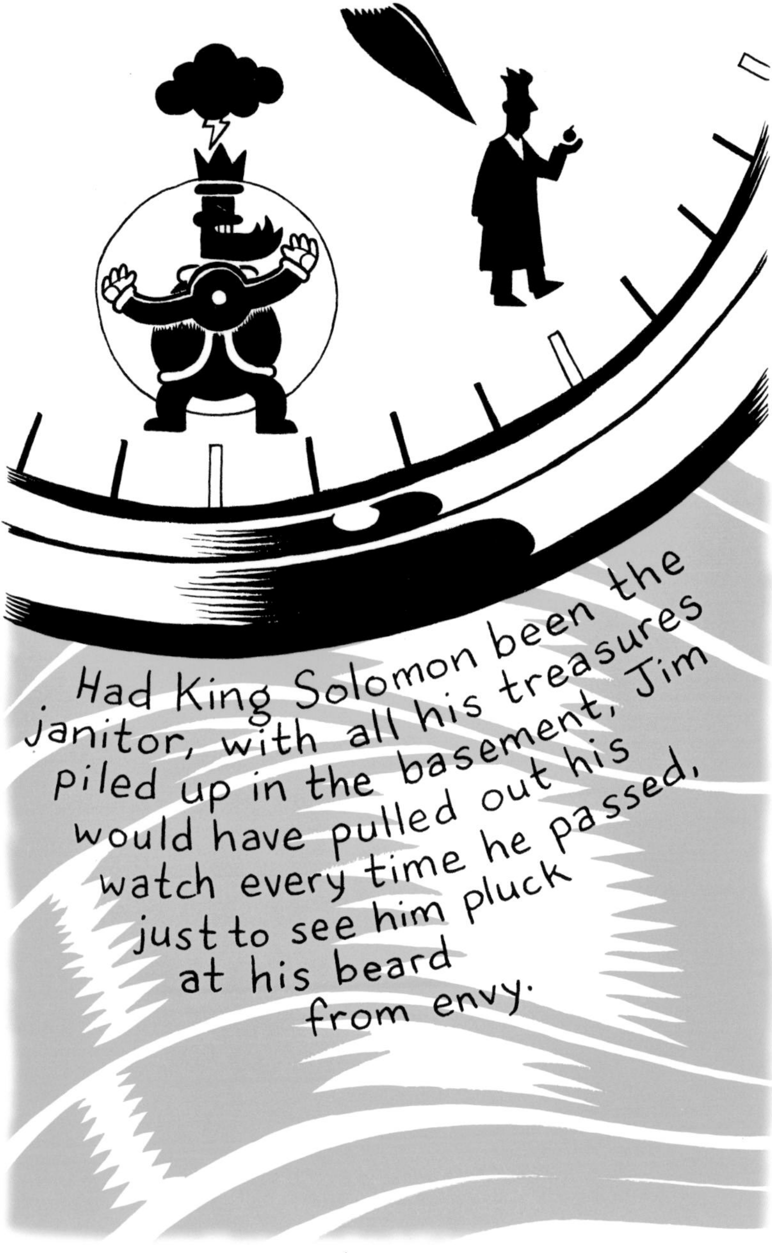
Had King Solomon been the janitor, with all his treasures piled up in the basement, Jim would have pulled out his watch every time he passed, just to see him pluck at his beard from envy.

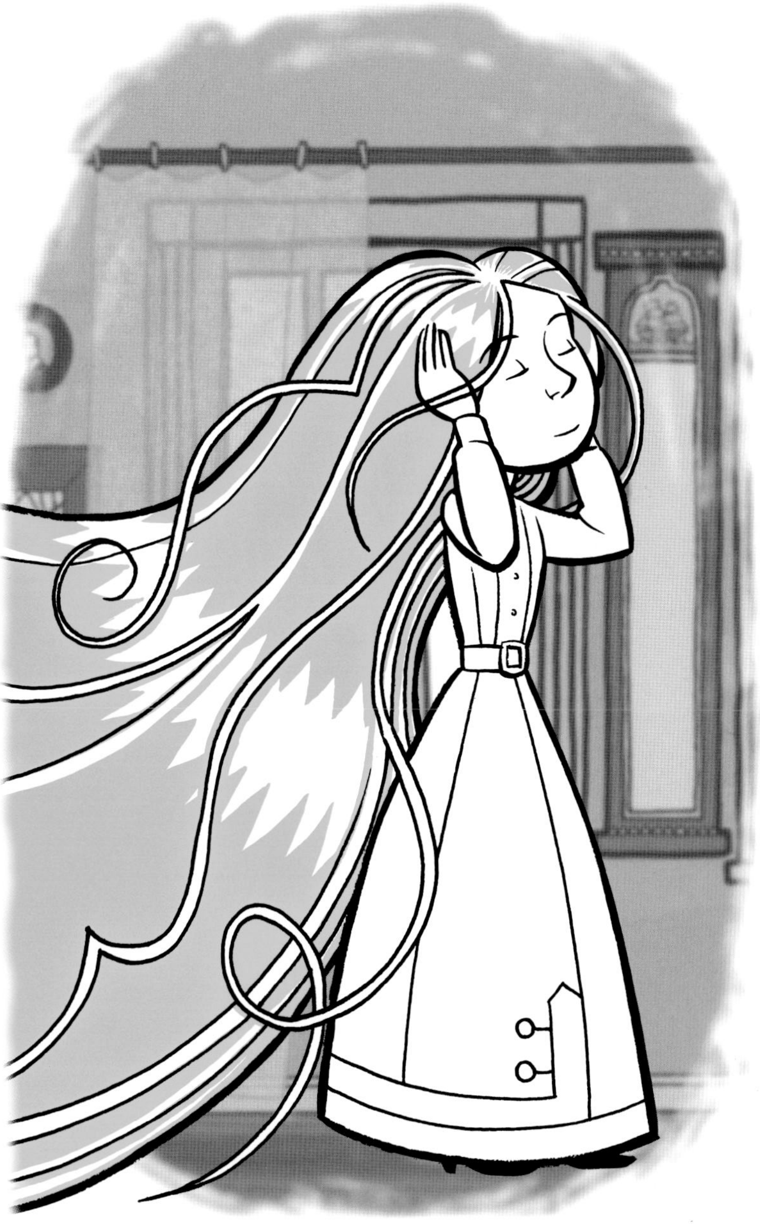

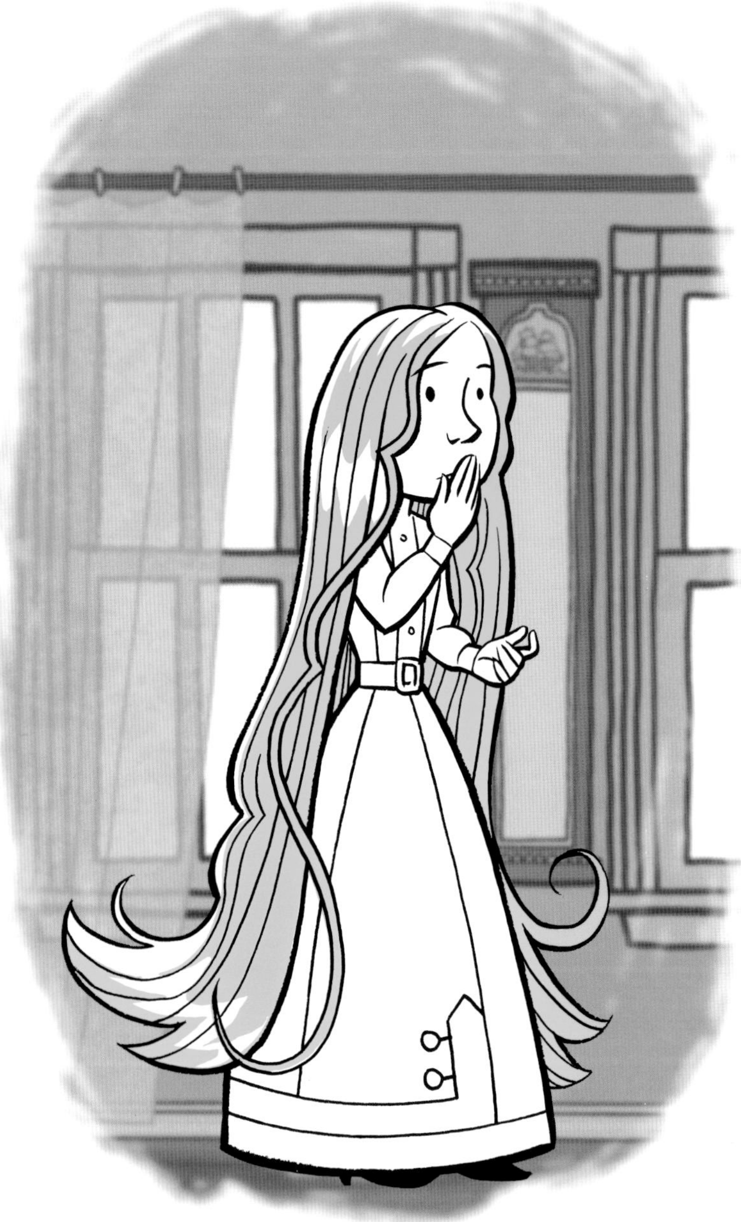

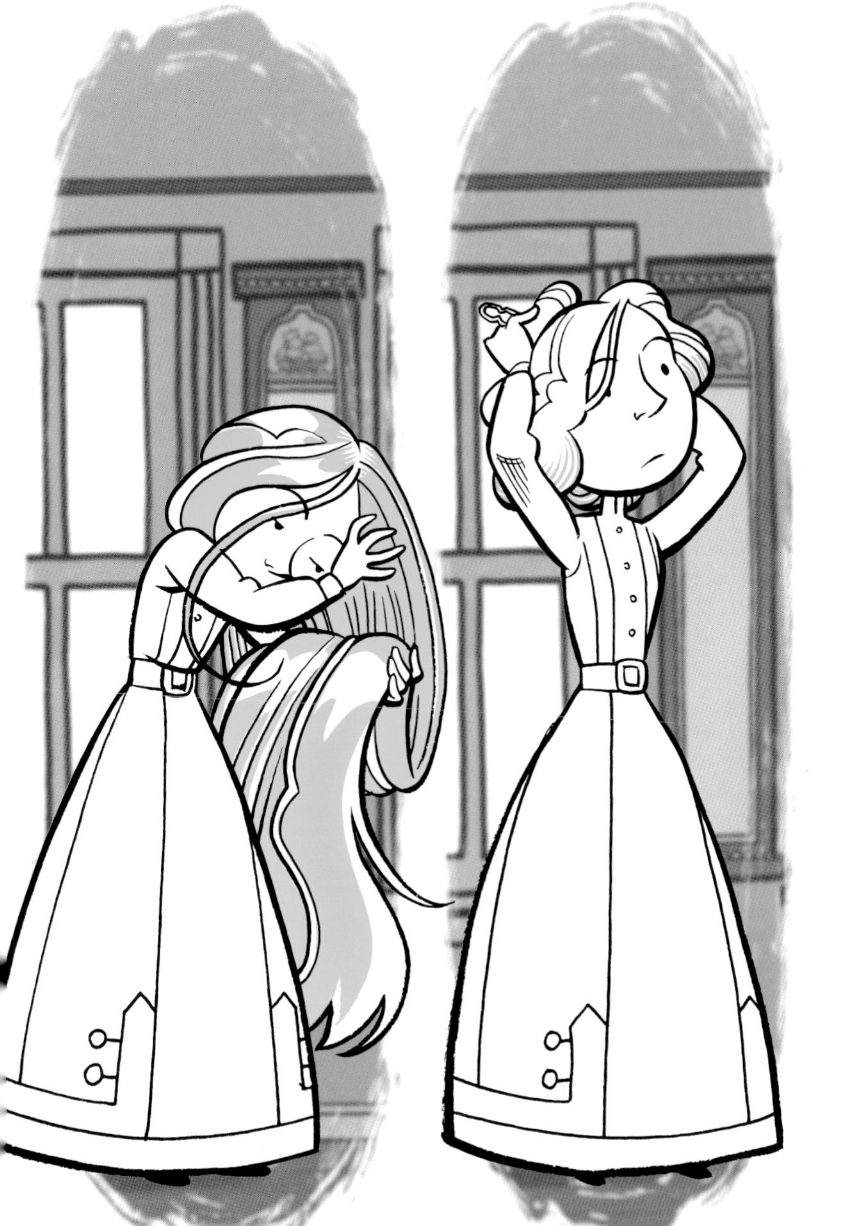

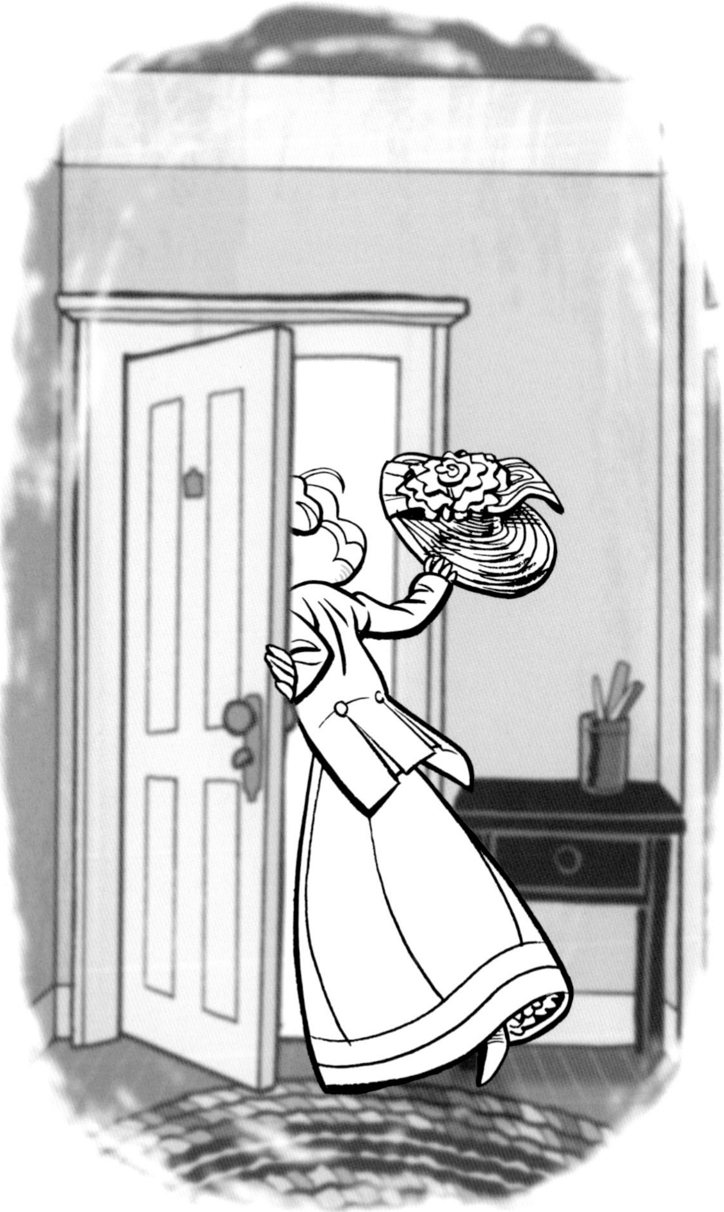

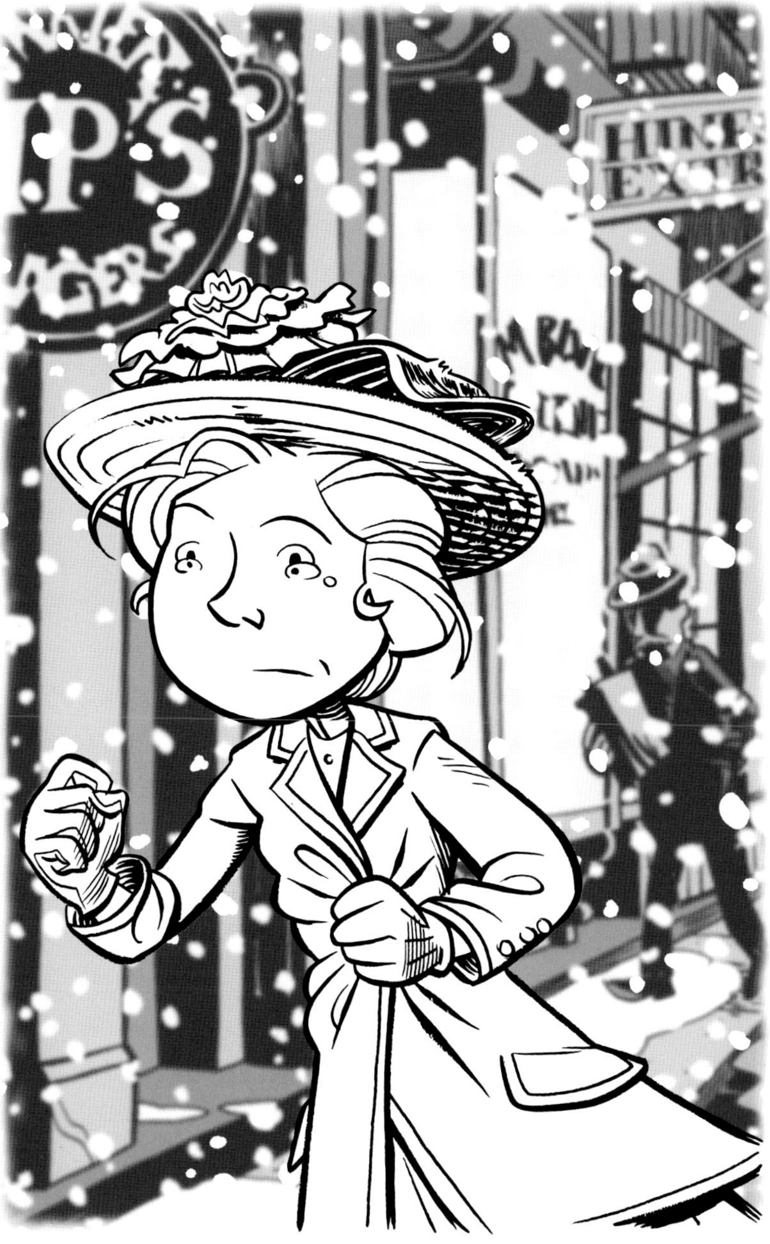

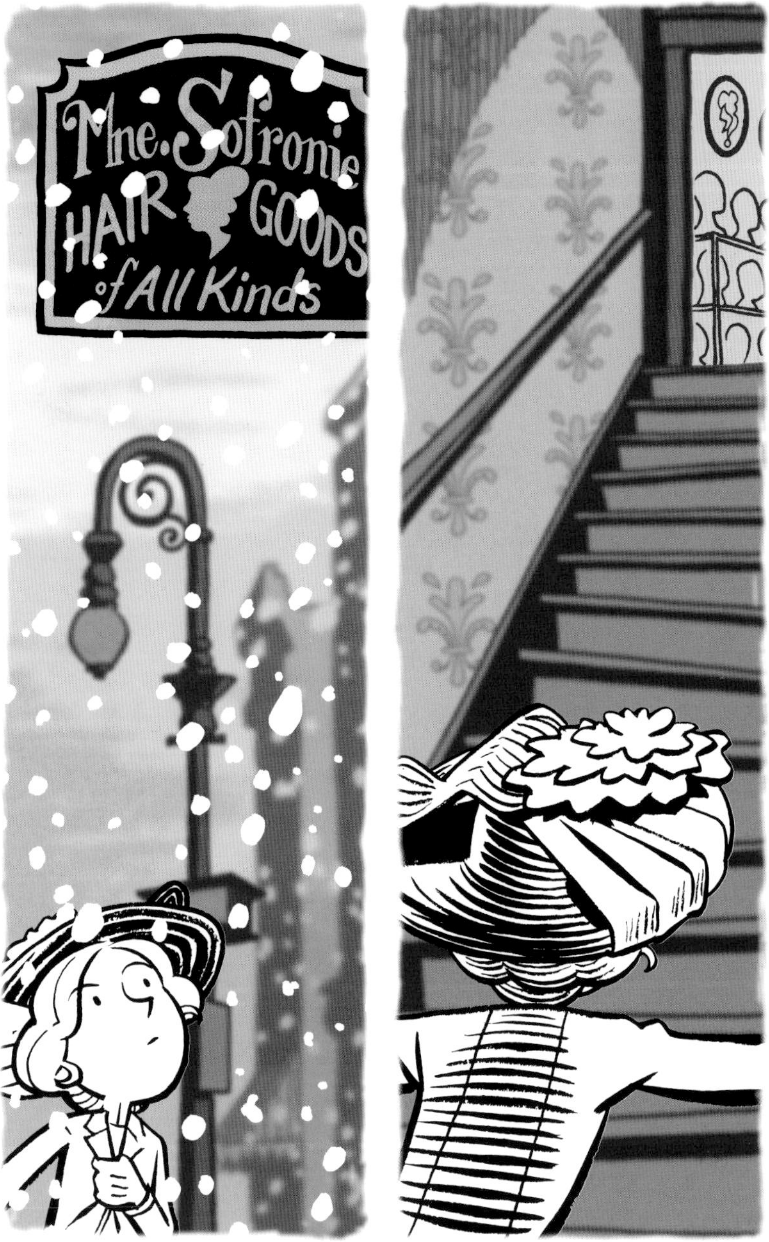
Mme. Sofronie
HAIR GOODS
of All Kinds

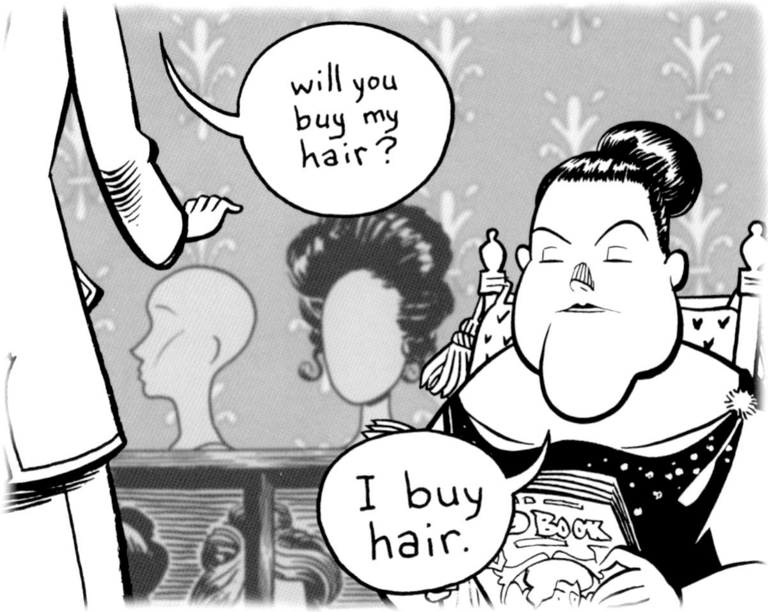
will you buy my hair?
I buy hair.

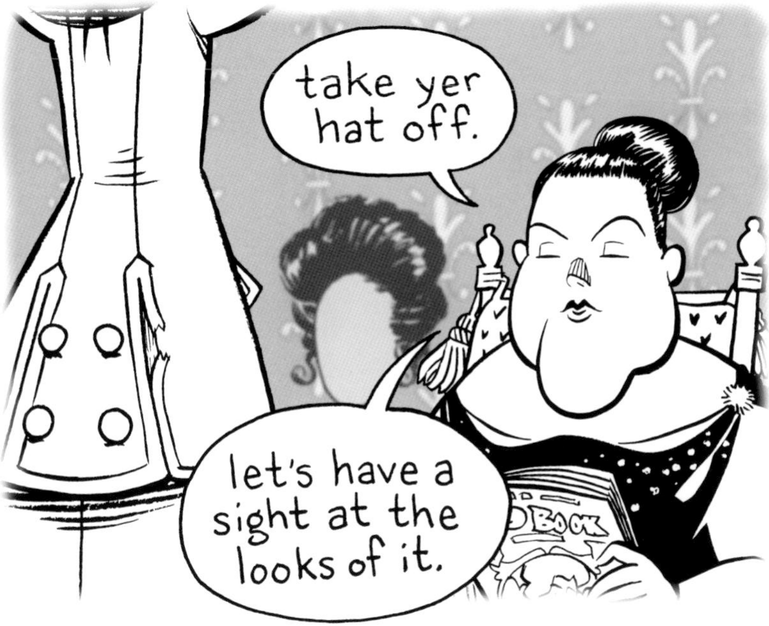
take yer hat off.
let's have a sight at the looks of it.

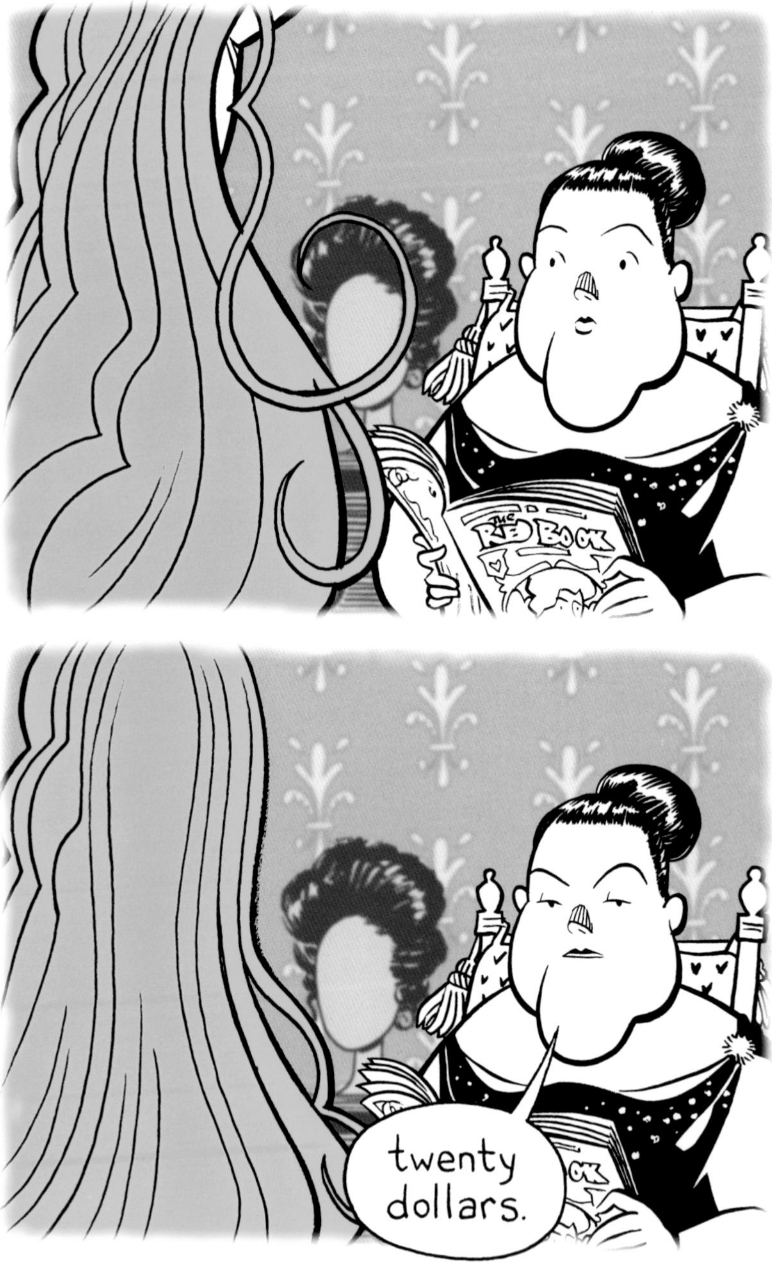
THE RED BOOK
twenty dollars.

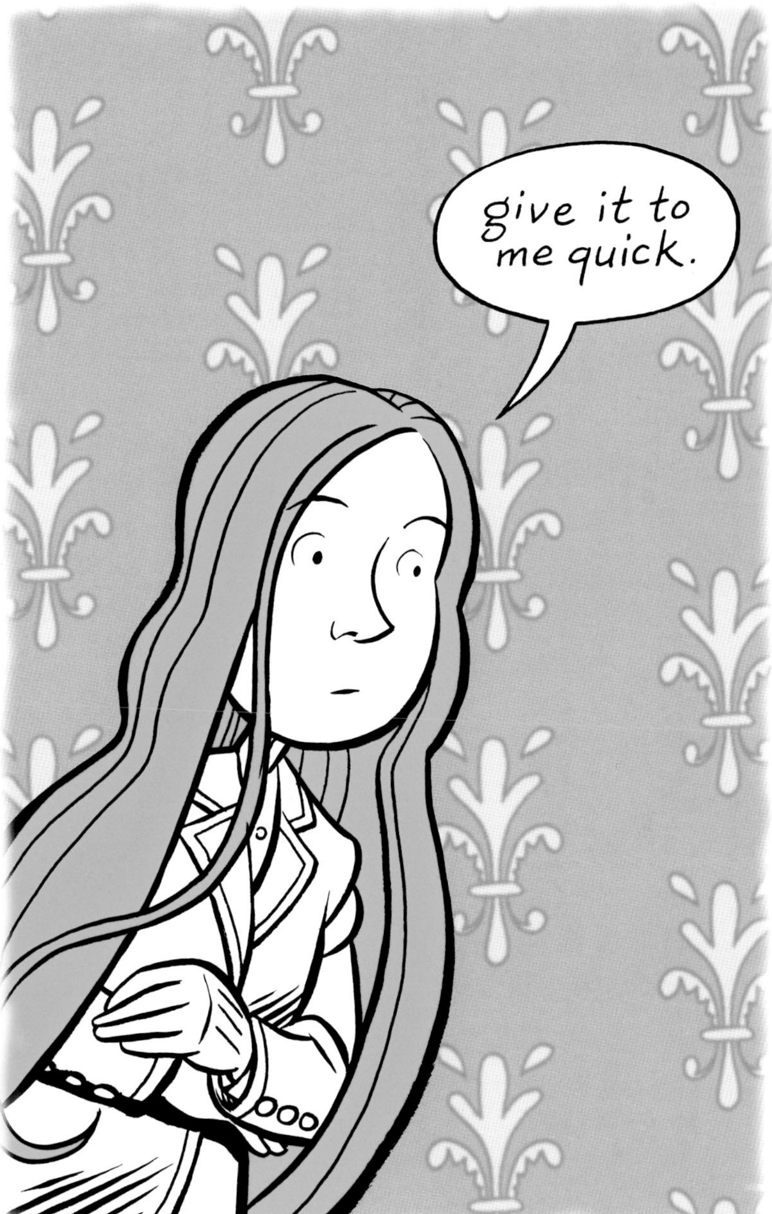
give it to me quick.

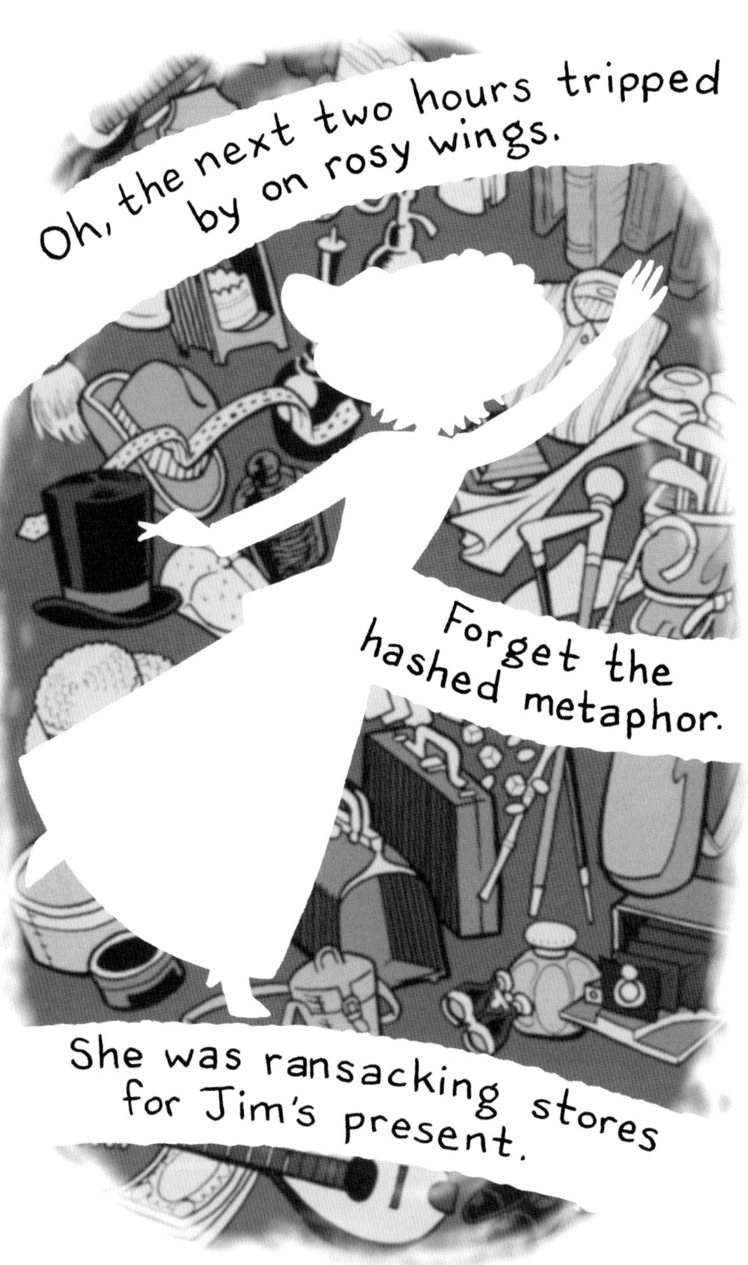
Oh, the next two hours tripped by on rosy wings.
Forget the hashed metaphor.
She was ransacking stores for Jim's present.

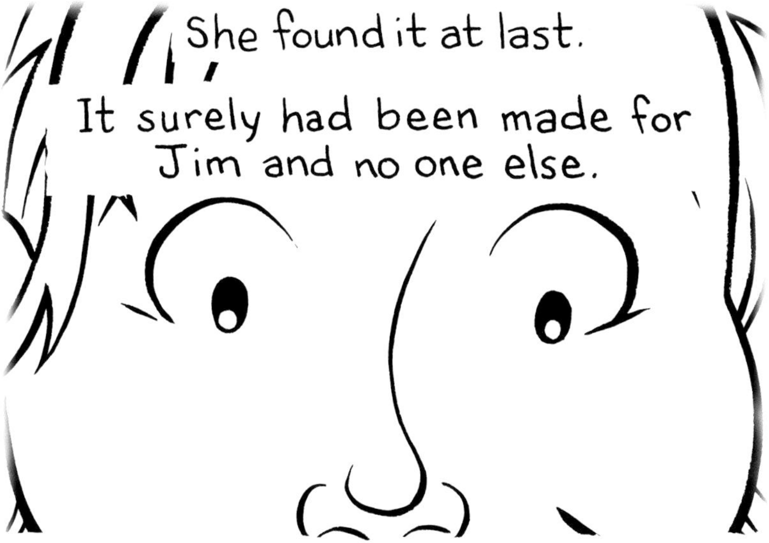
She found it at last.
It surely had been made for Jim and no one else.

Simple and chaste in design, properly proclaiming its value by substance alone and not by meretricious ornamentation—

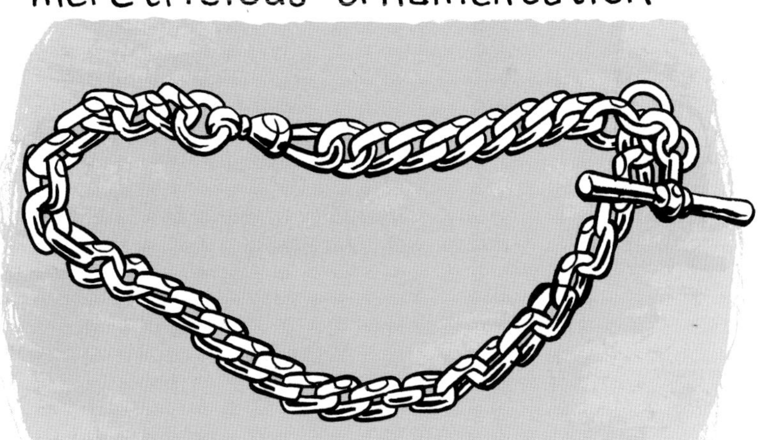

as all good things should do.

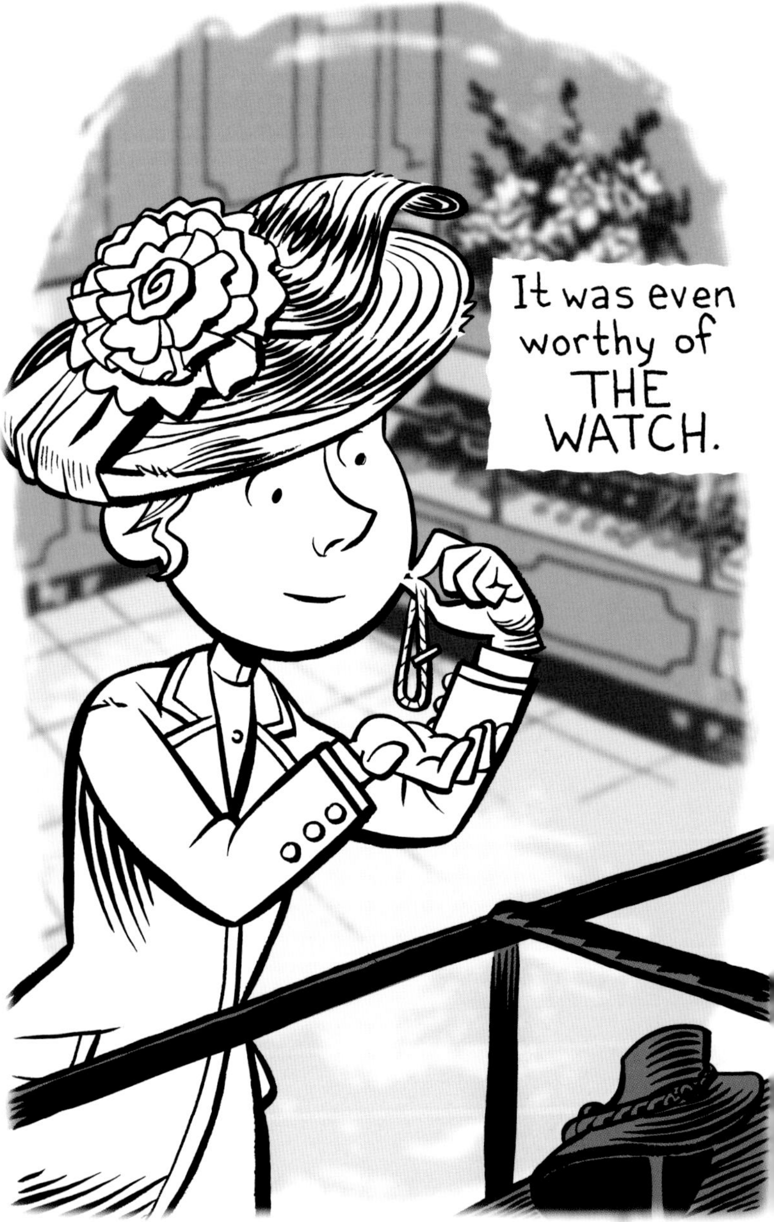
It was even worthy of THE WATCH.

Twenty-one dollars they took from her for it, and she hurried home with the 87 cents.

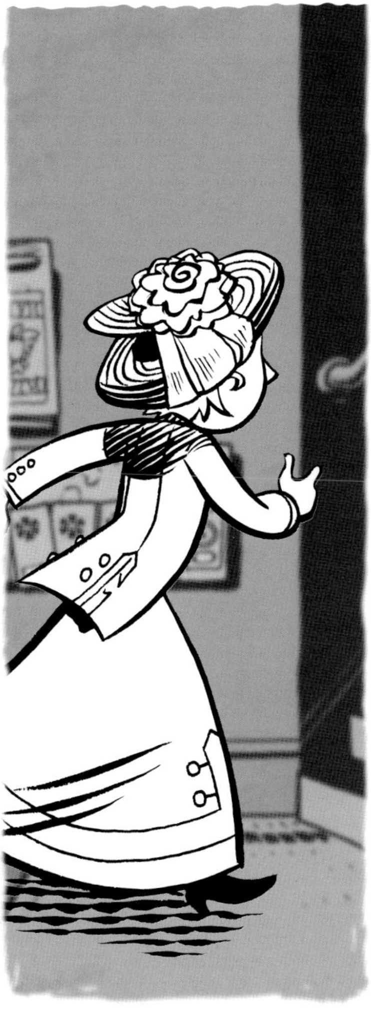

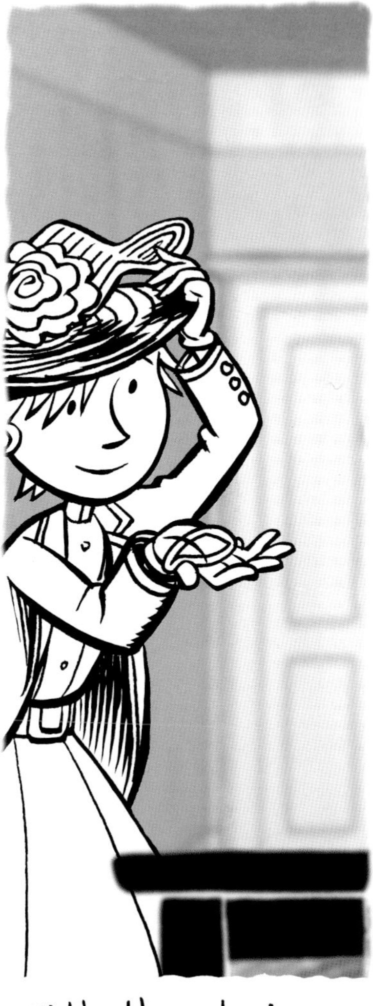

With the chain on his watch Jim might be properly anxious about the time in any company.

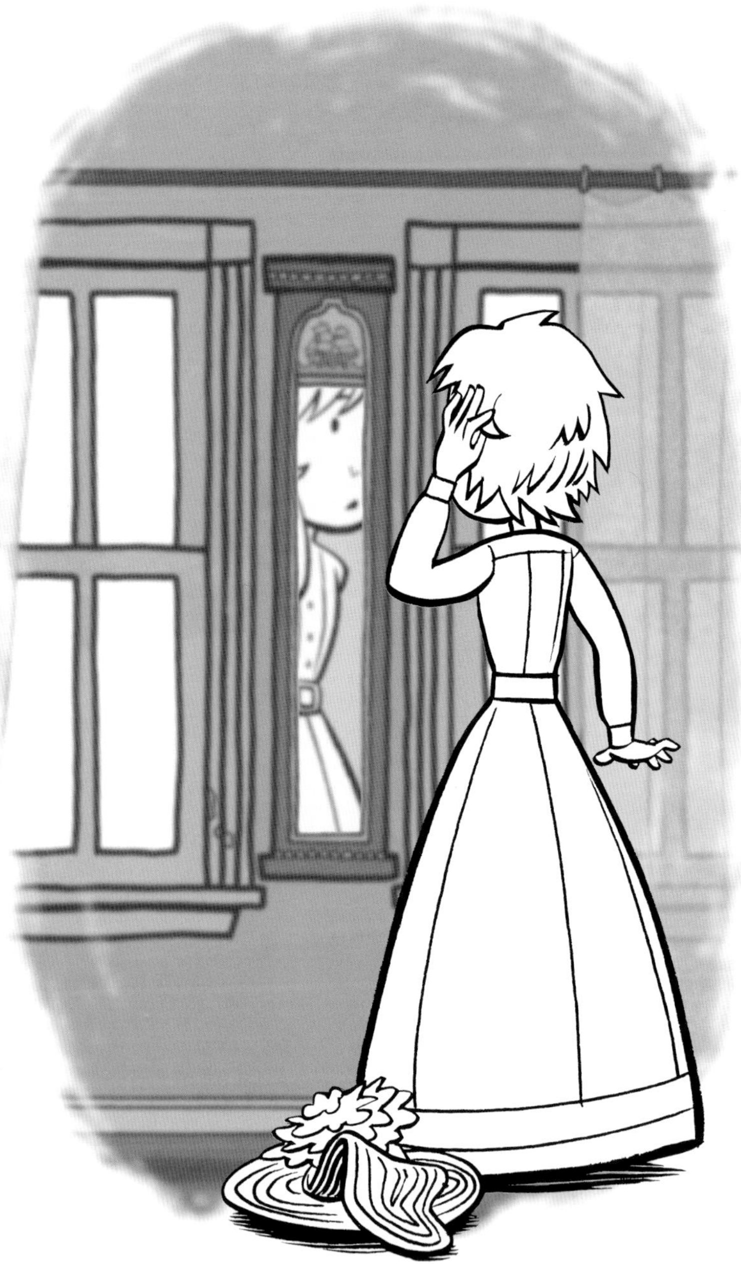

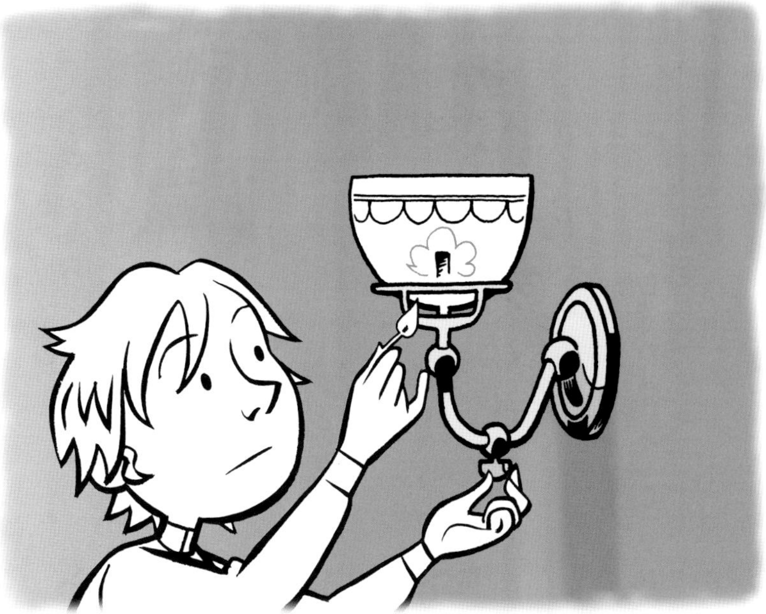

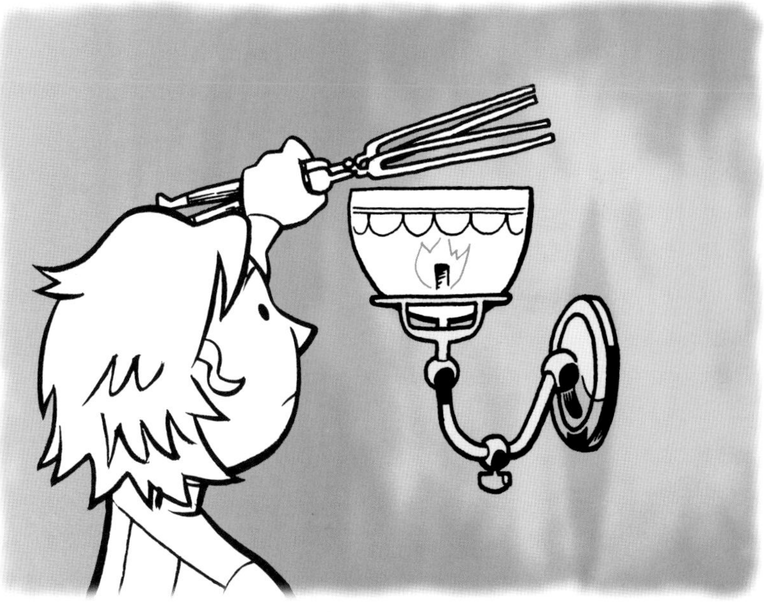

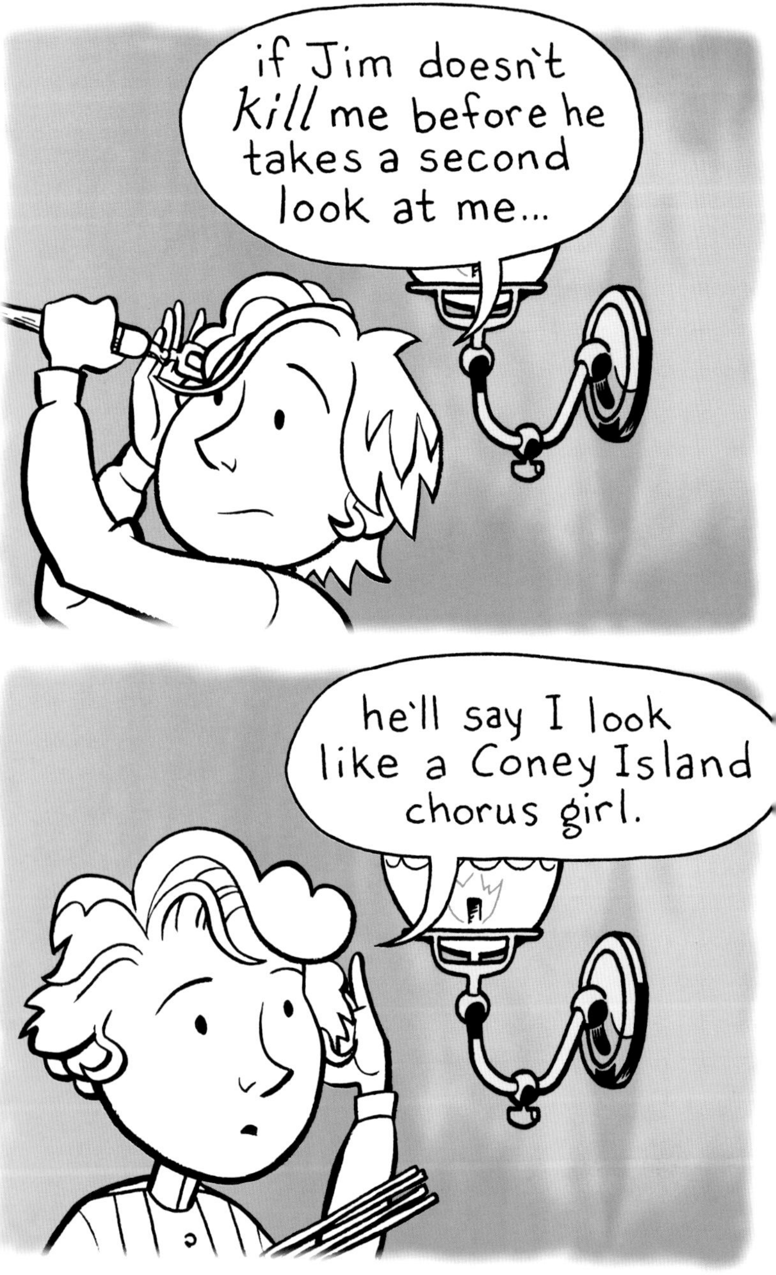
if Jim doesn't *kill* me before he takes a second look at me...
he'll say I look like a Coney Island chorus girl.

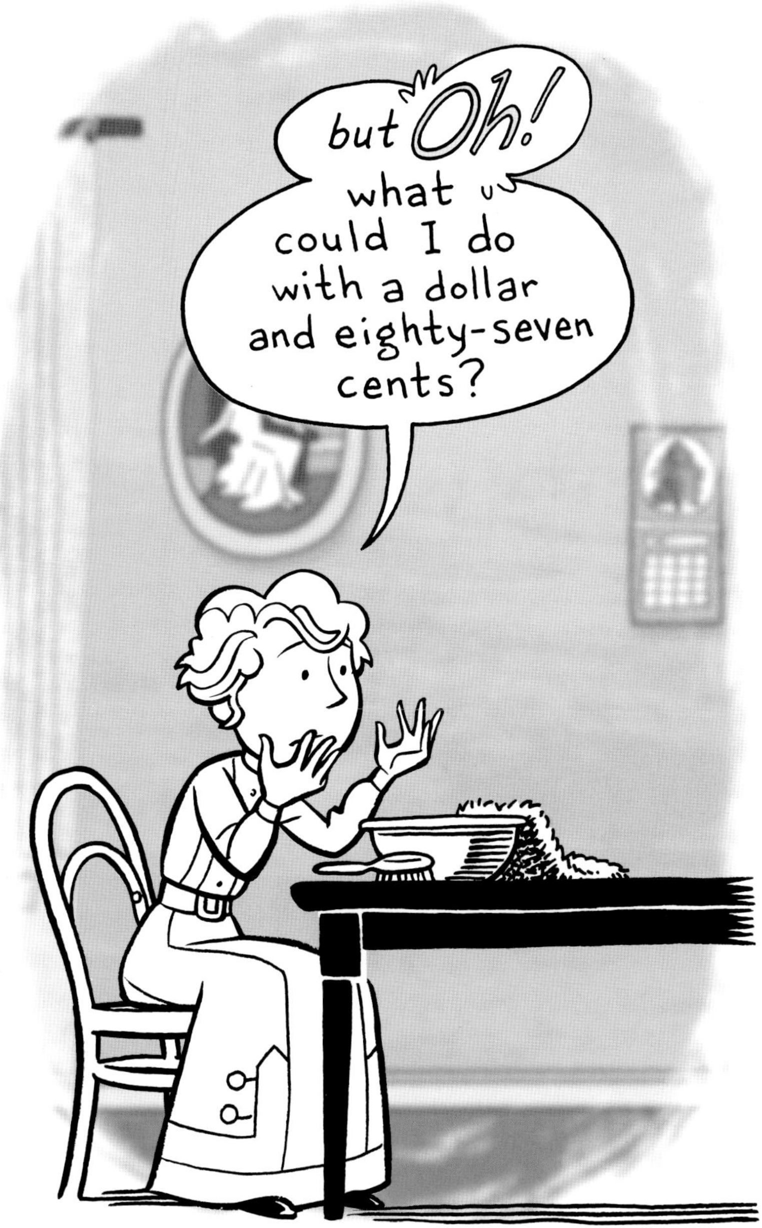
but Oh! what could I do with a dollar and eighty-seven cents?

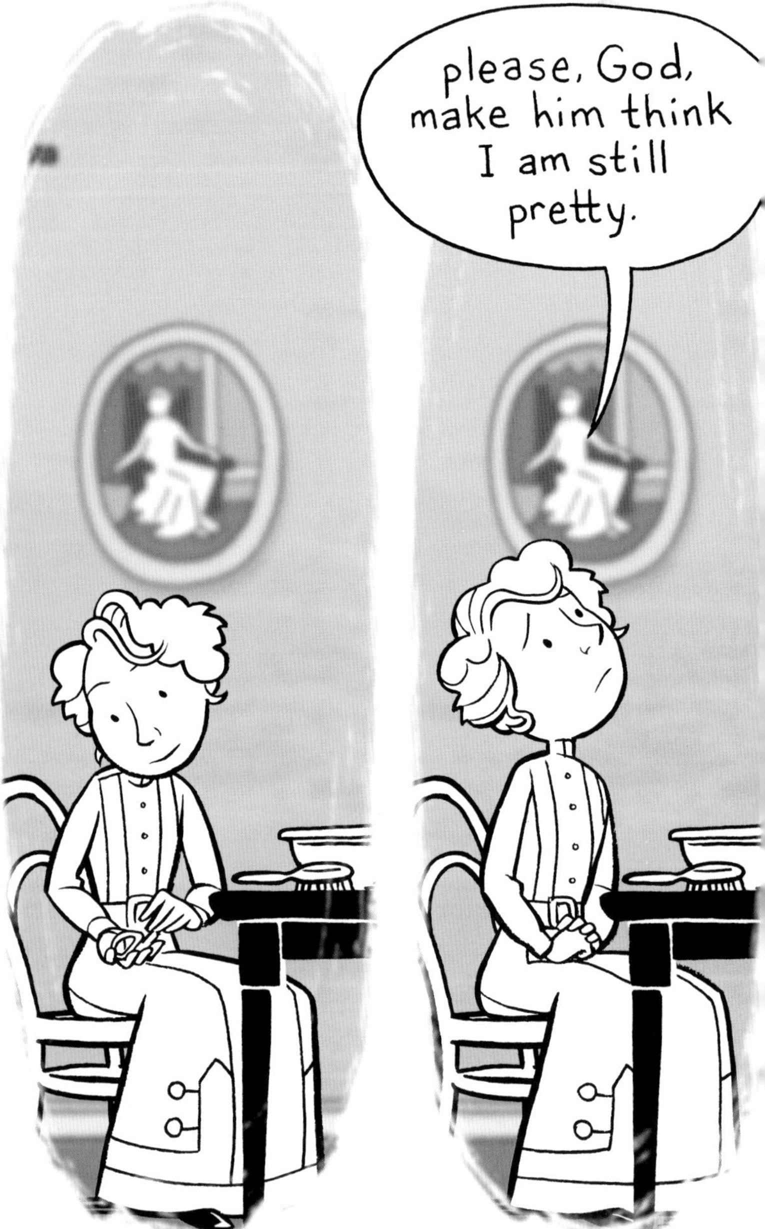
please, God, make him think I am still pretty.

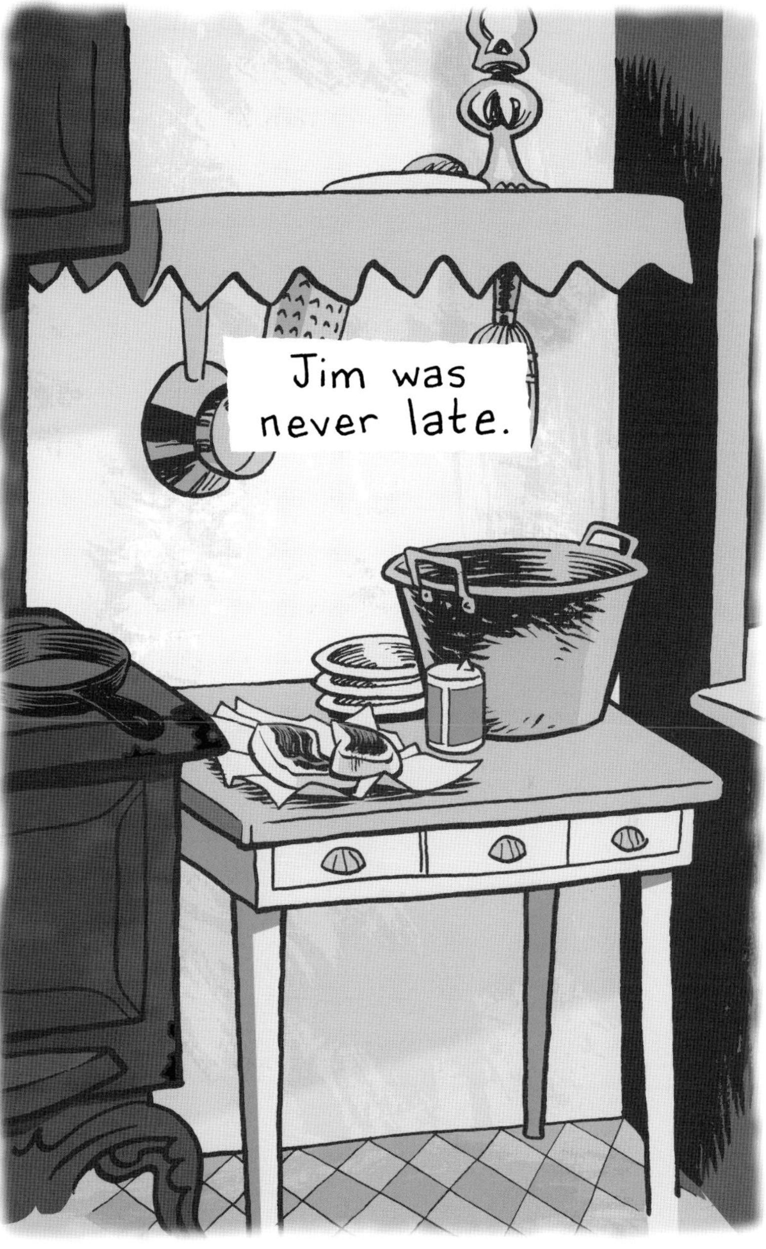
Jim was
never late.

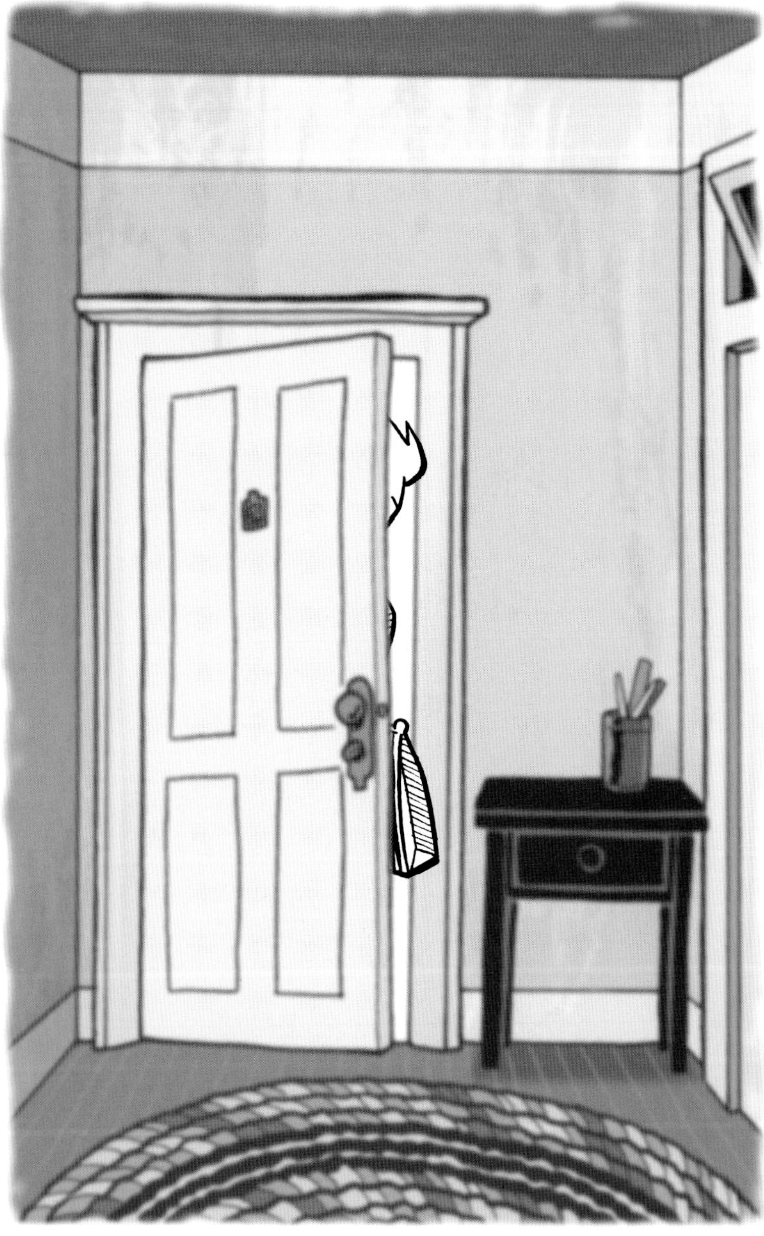

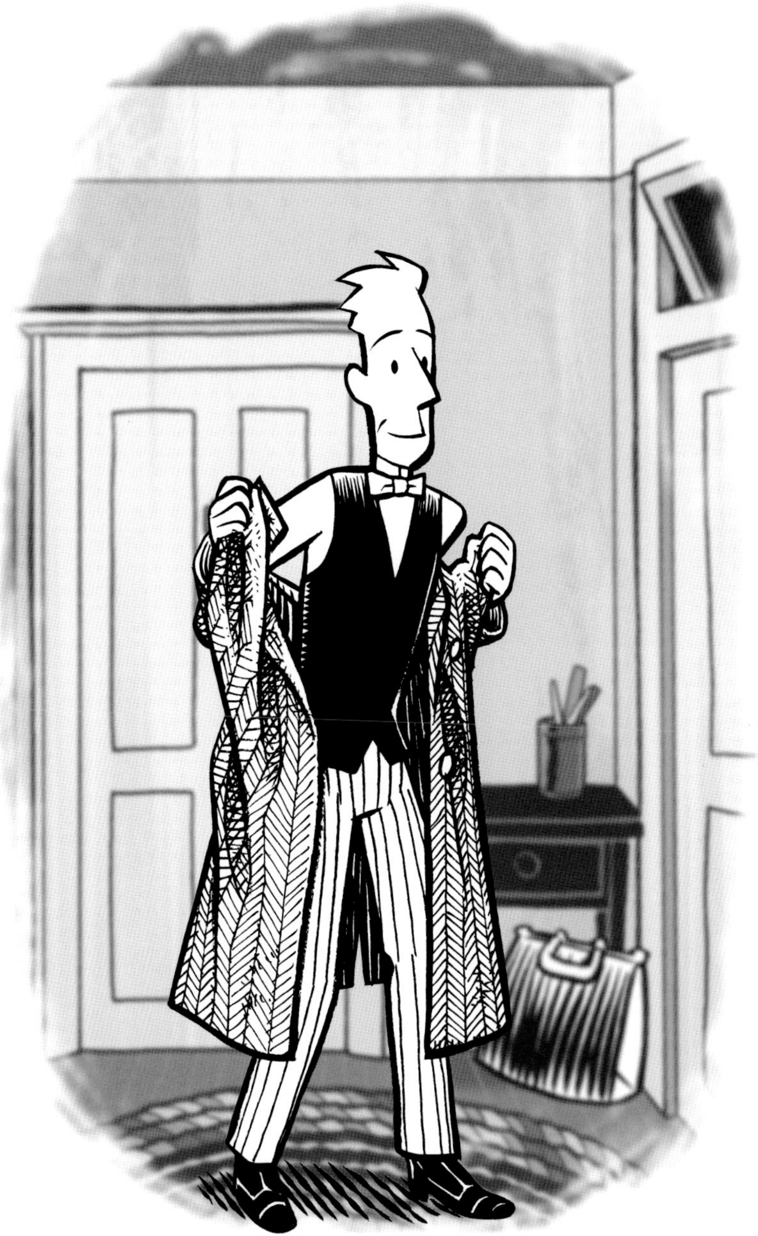

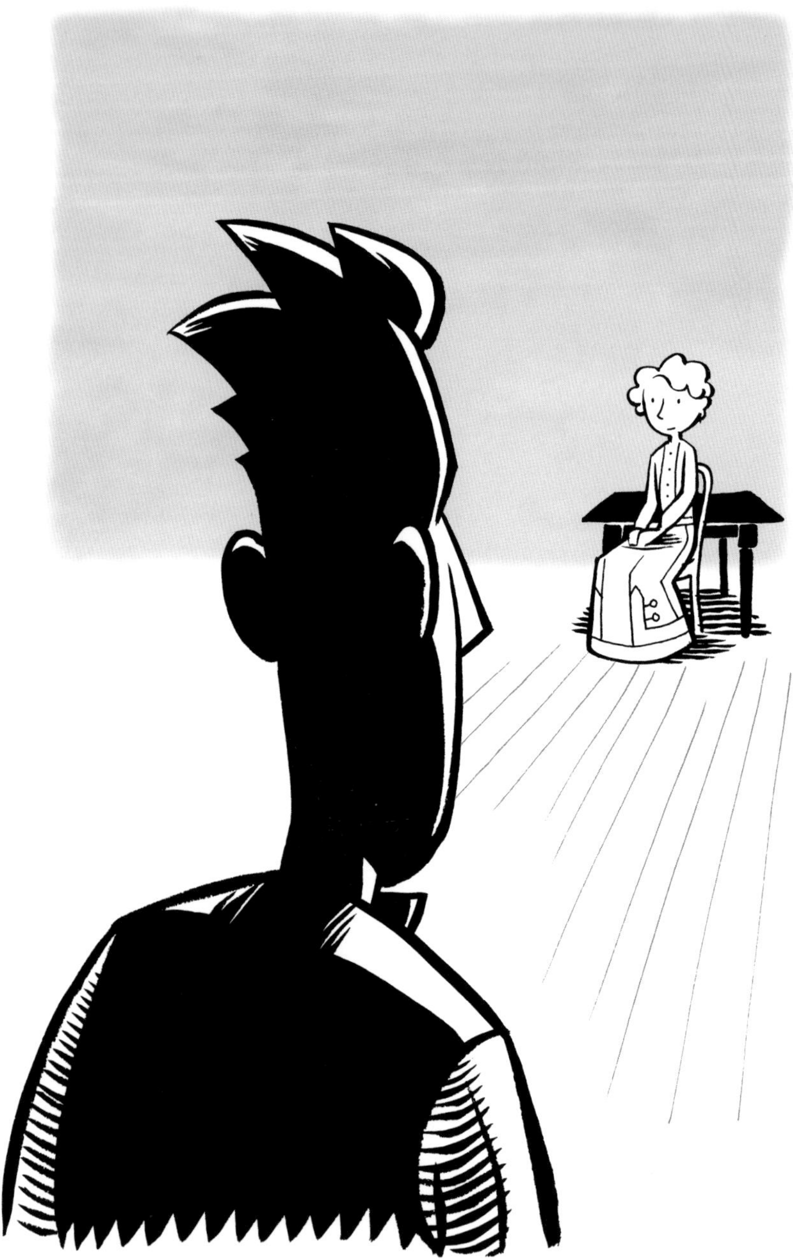

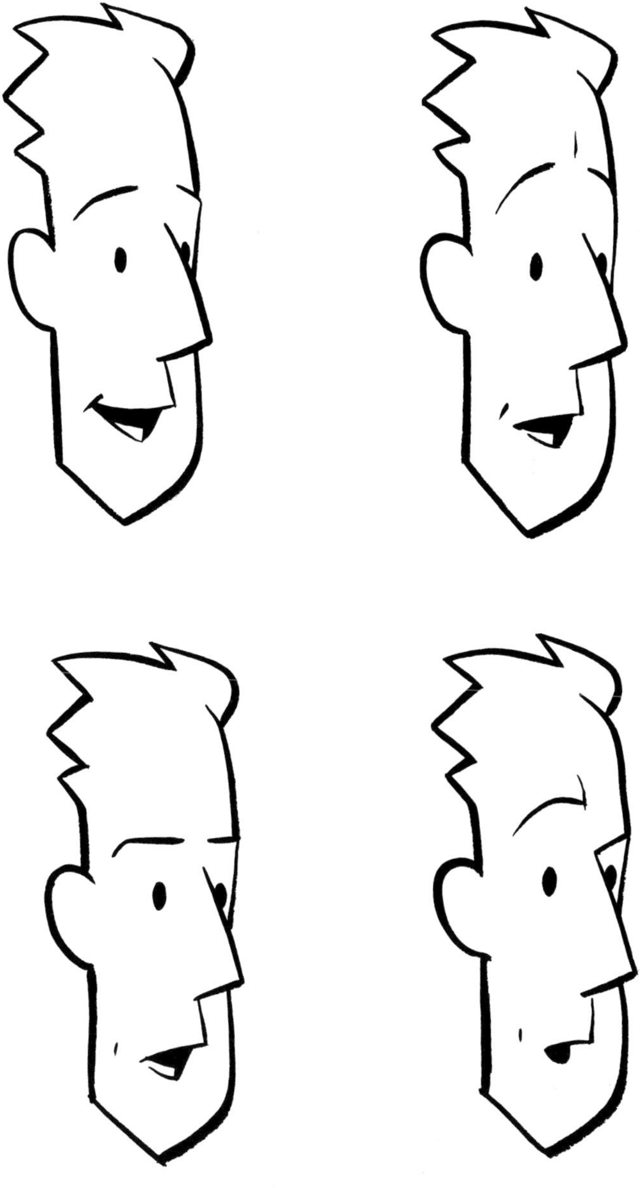

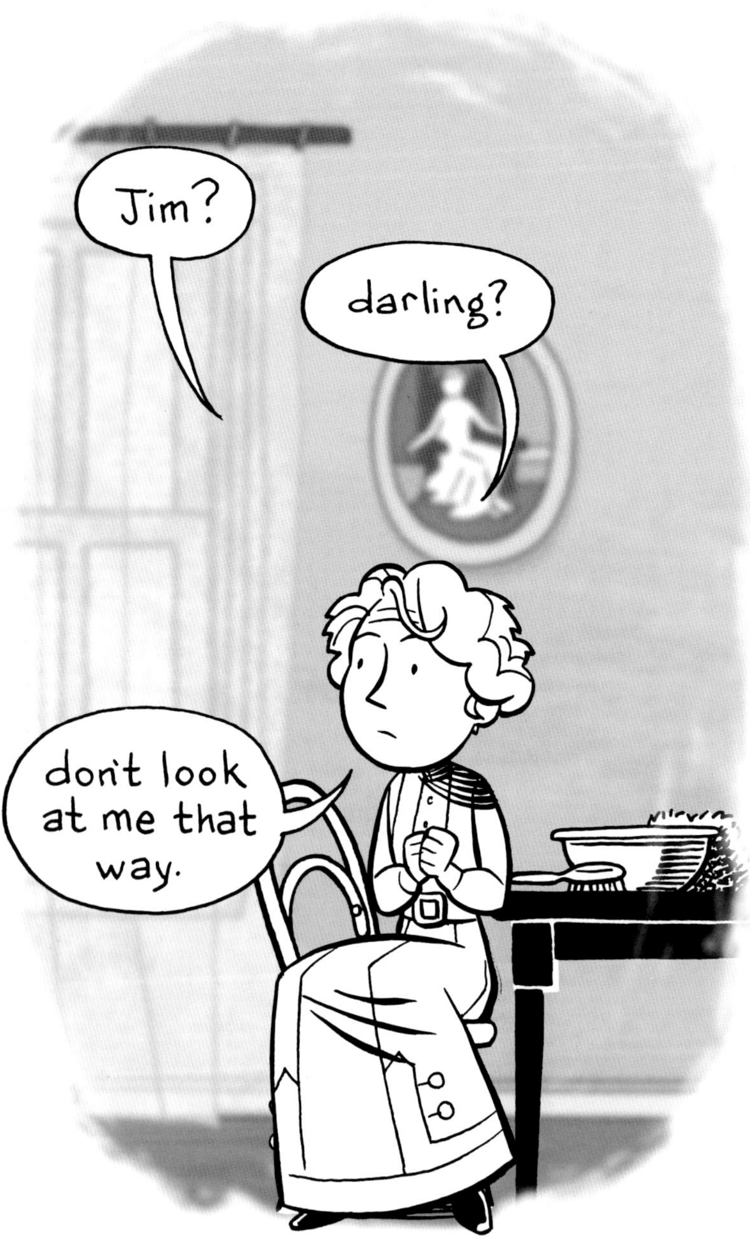
Jim?
darling?
don't look at me that way.

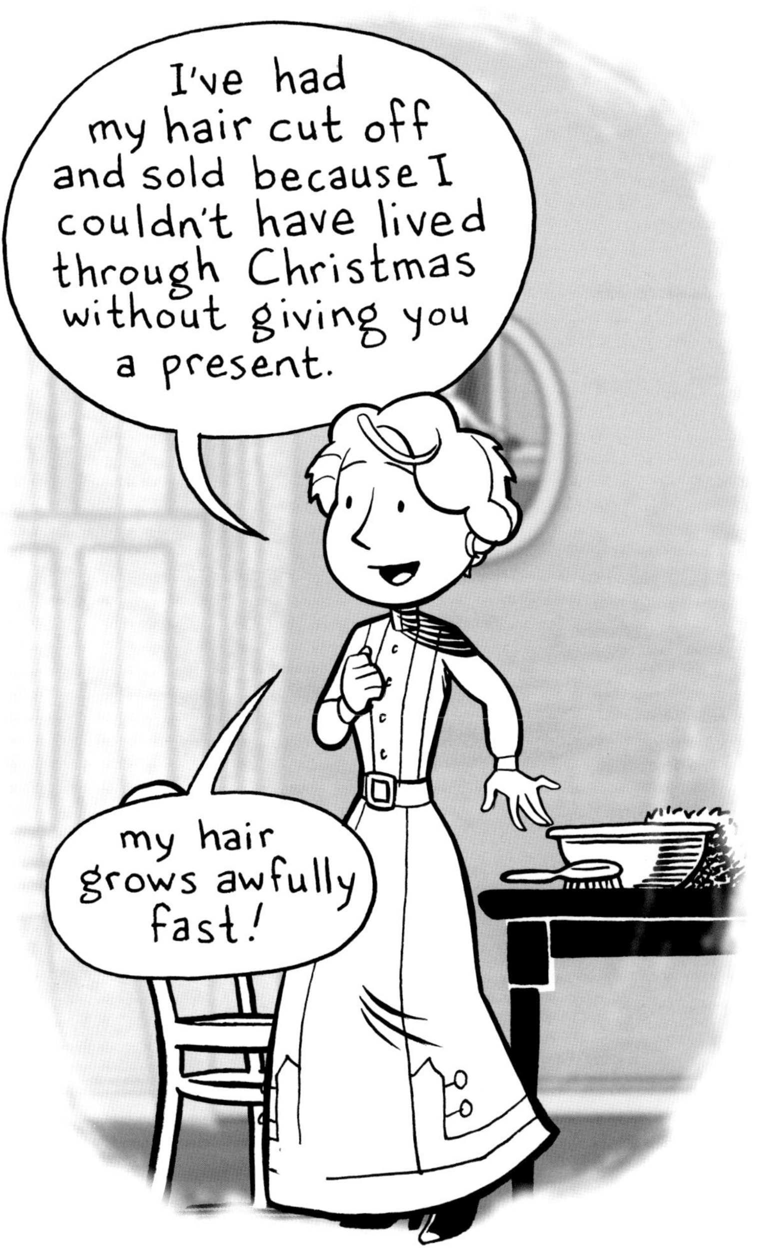
I've had my hair cut off and sold because I couldn't have lived through Christmas without giving you a present.
my hair grows awfully fast!

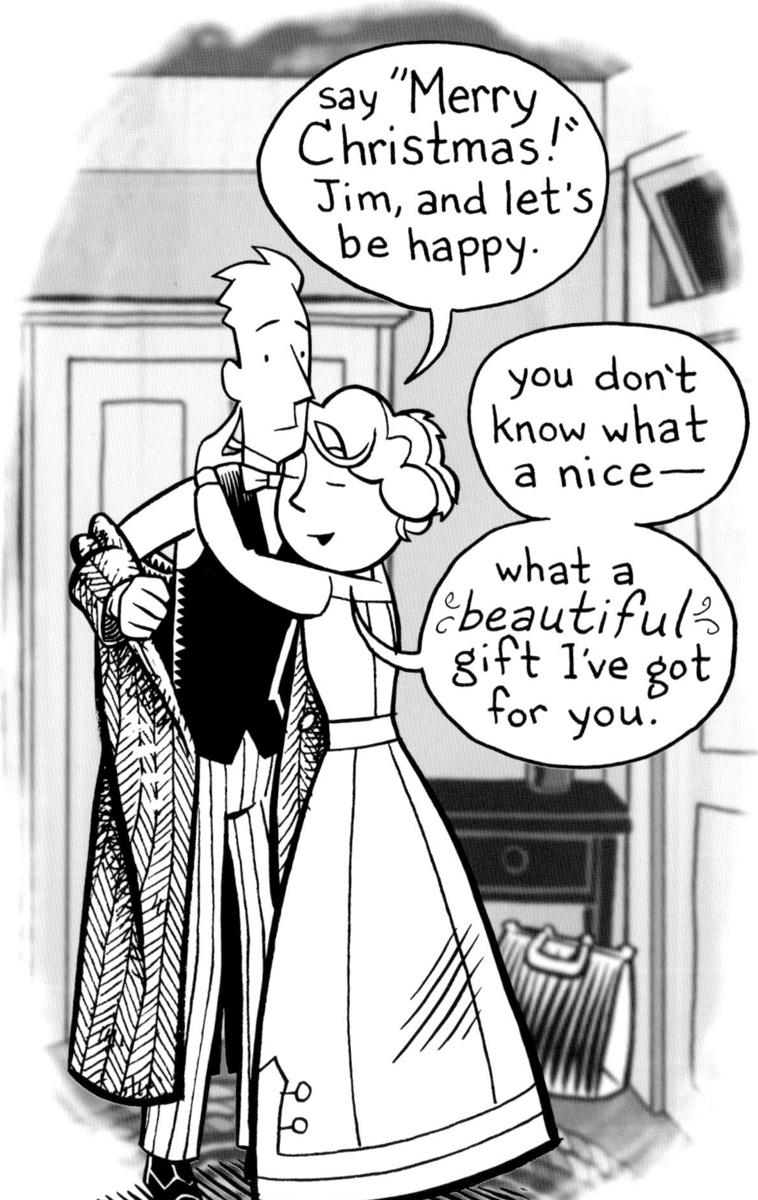
say "Merry Christmas!" Jim, and let's be happy.
you don't know what a nice—
what a beautiful gift I've got for you.

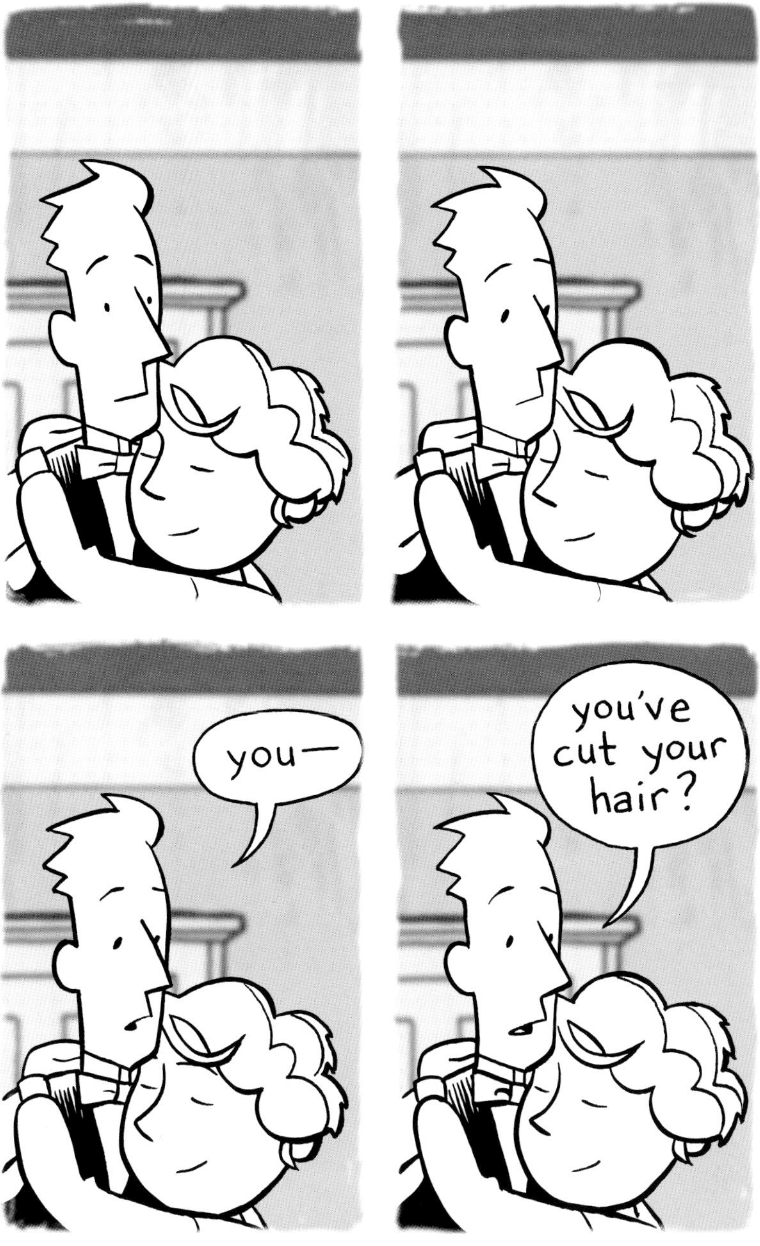
you—
you've cut your hair?

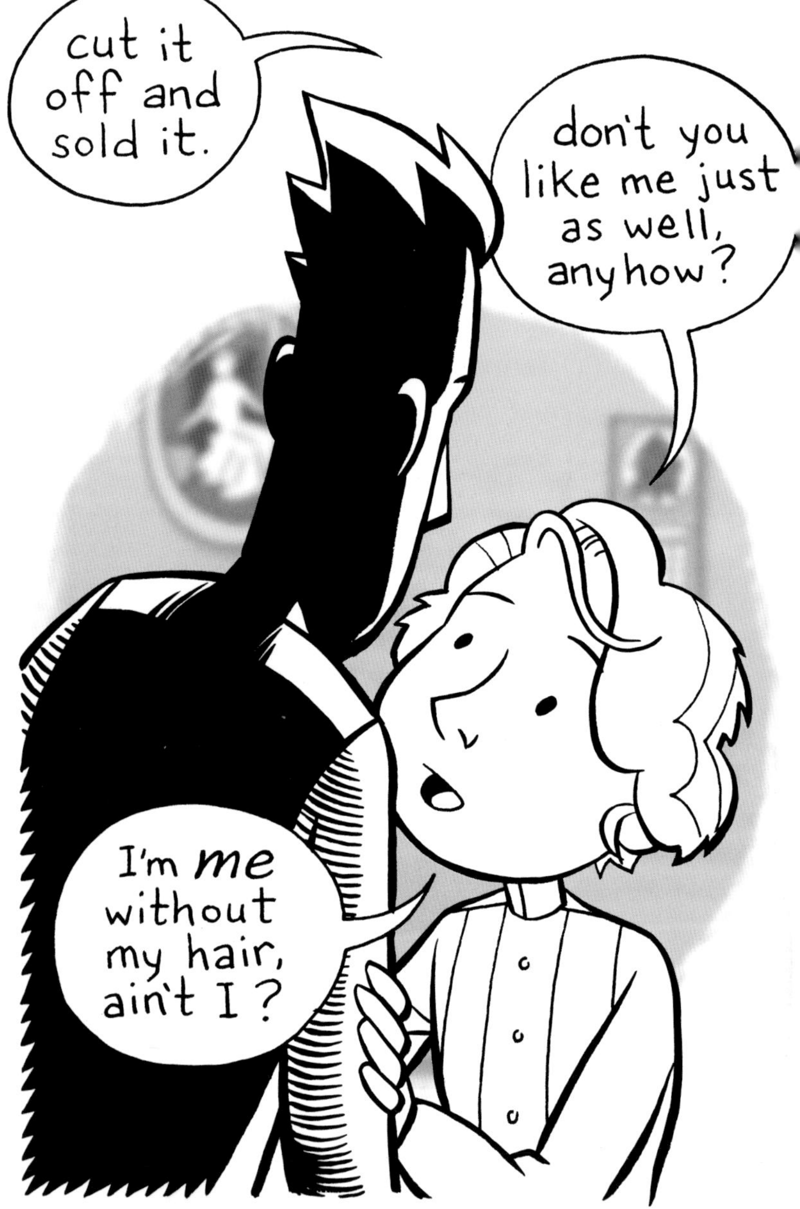
cut it off and sold it.
don't you like me just as well, anyhow?
I'm *me* without my hair, ain't I?

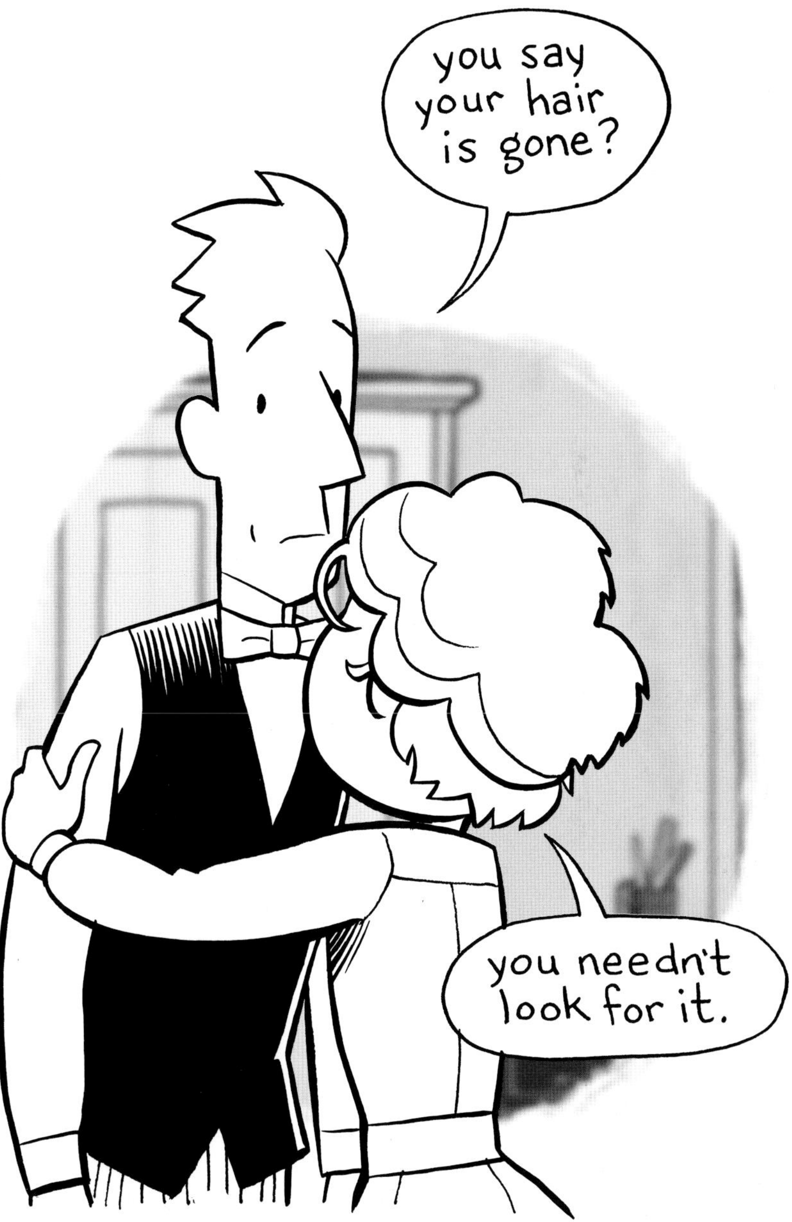
you say your hair is gone?
you needn't look for it.

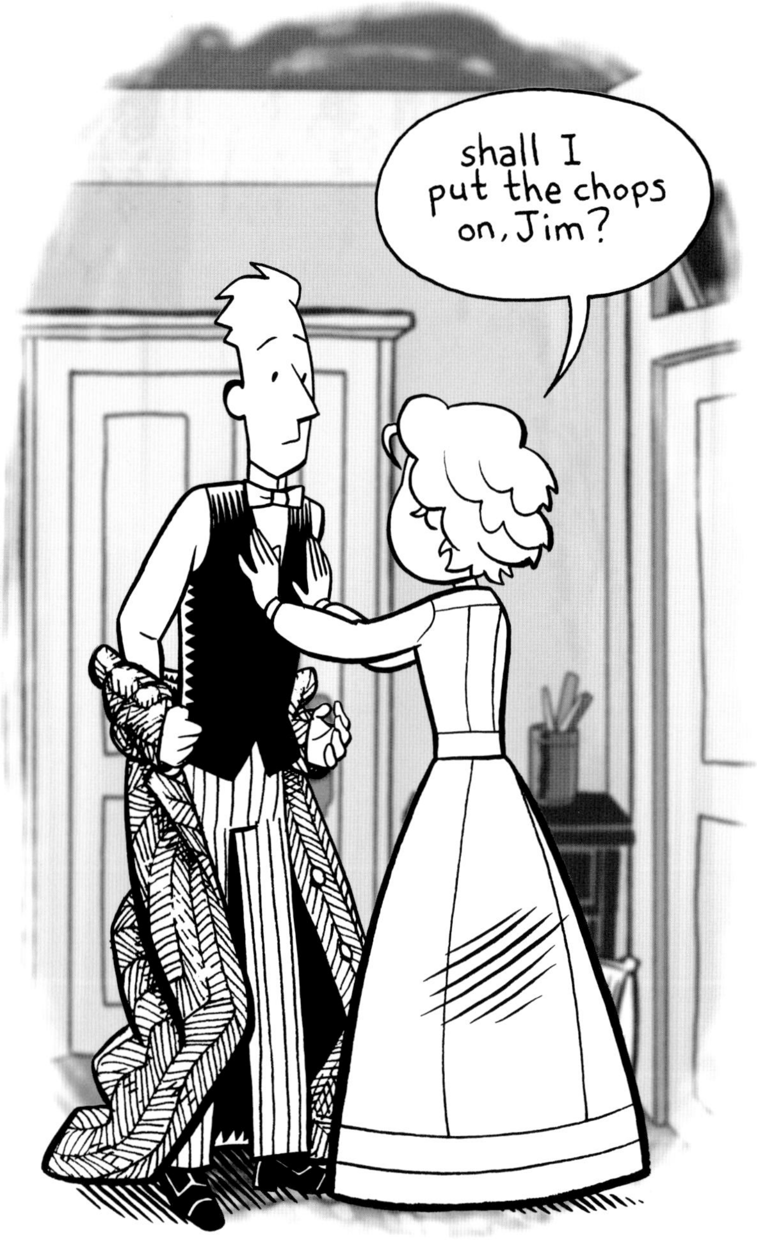
shall I put the chops on, Jim?

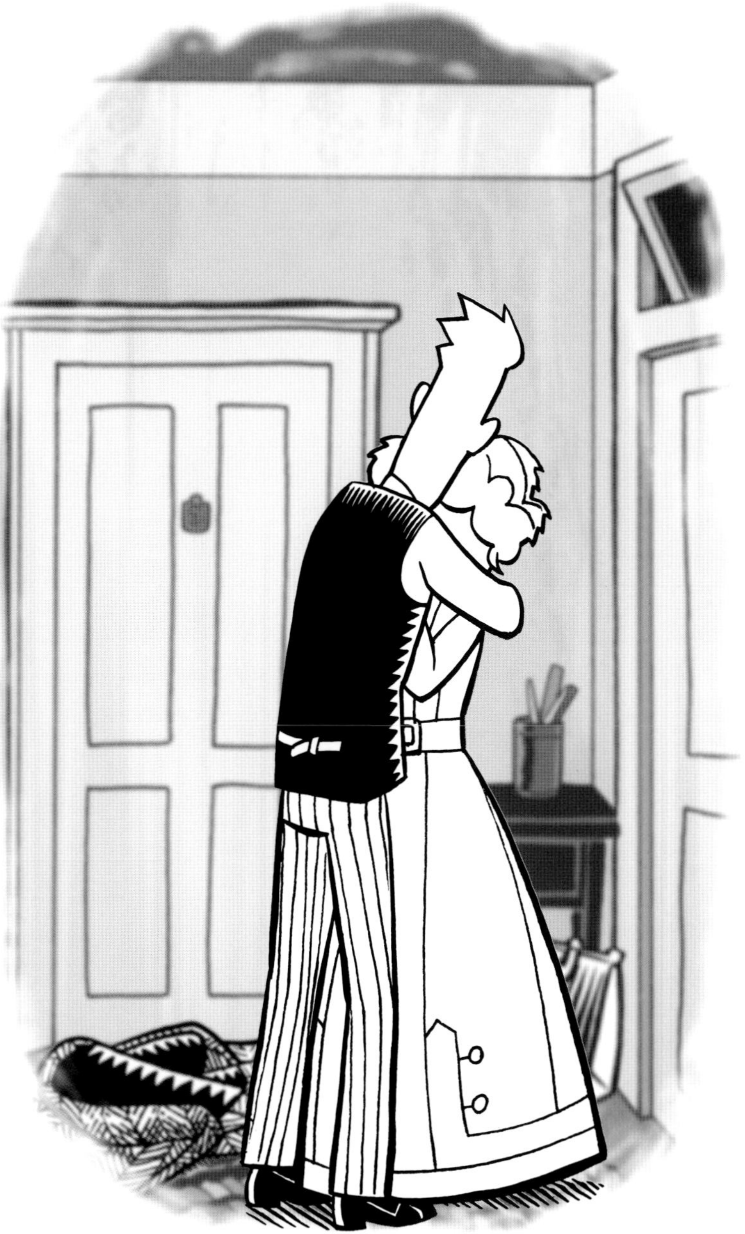

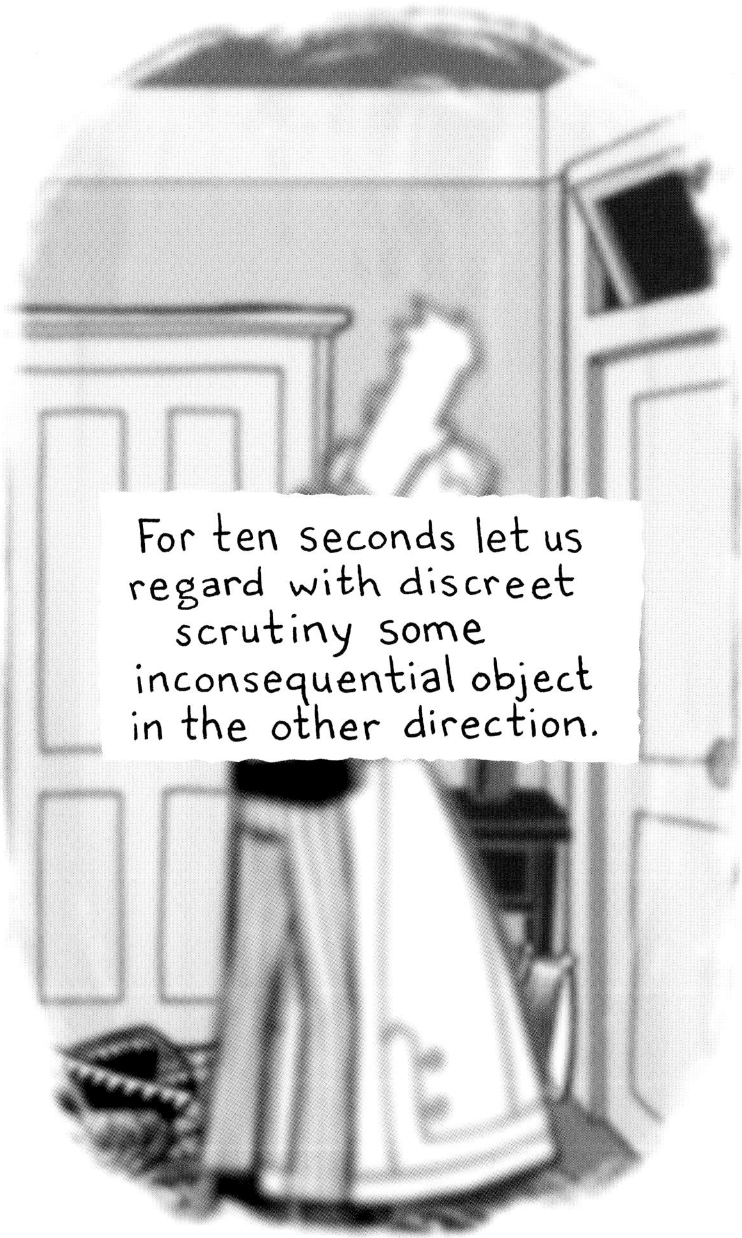
For ten seconds let us regard with discreet scrutiny some inconsequential object in the other direction.

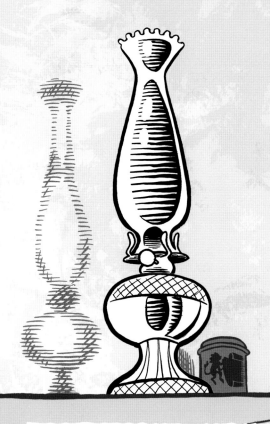

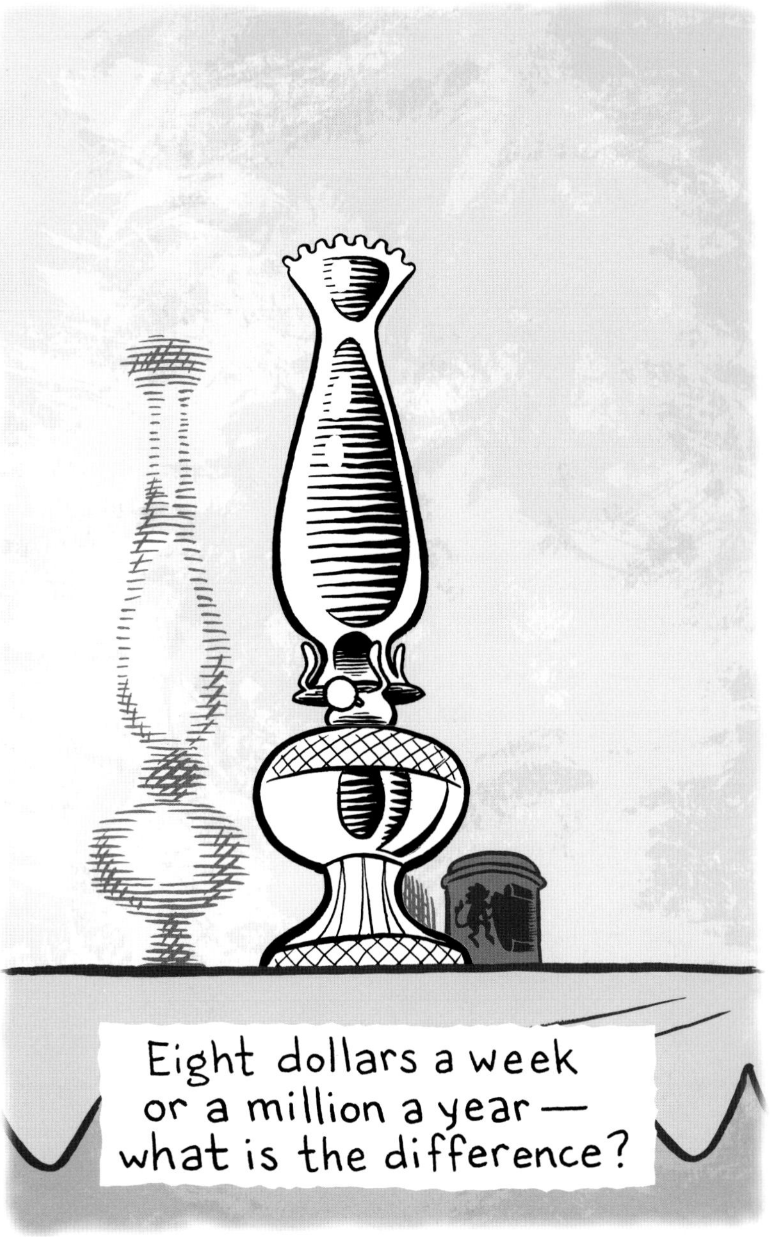

Eight dollars a week
or a million a year —
what is the difference?

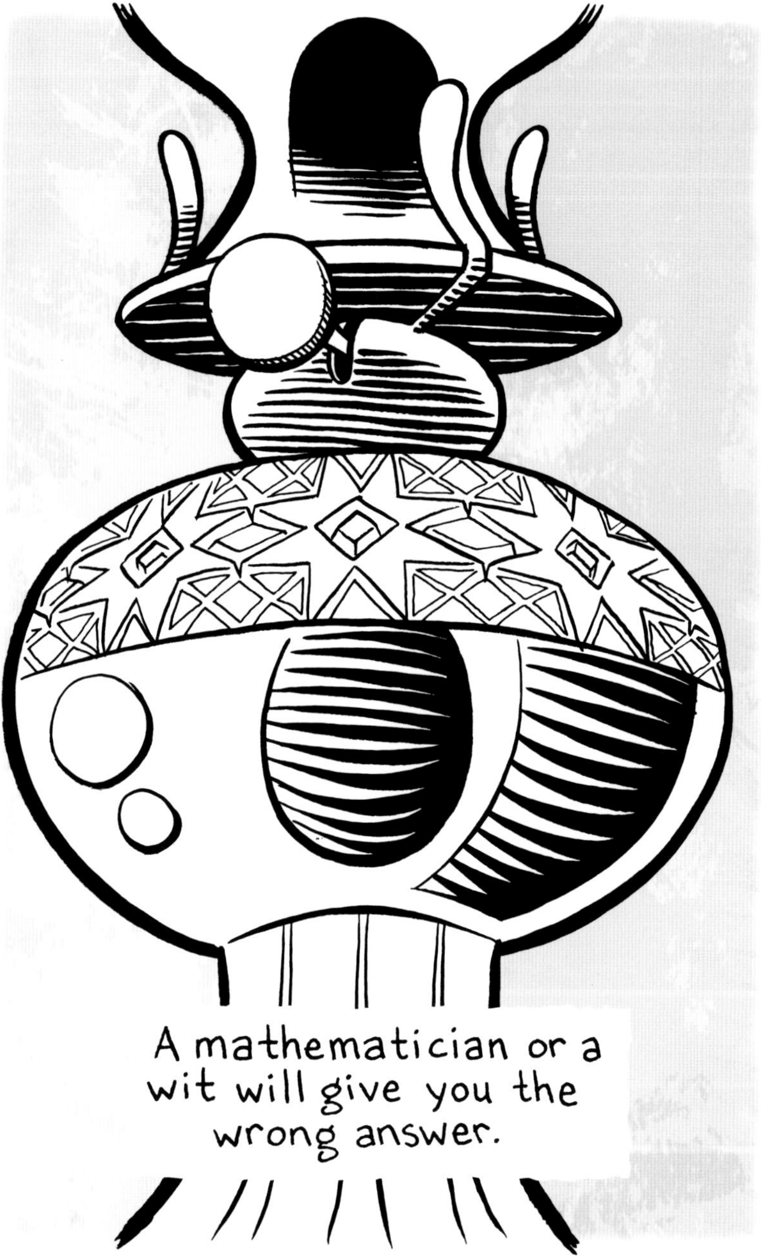
A mathematician or a wit will give you the wrong answer.

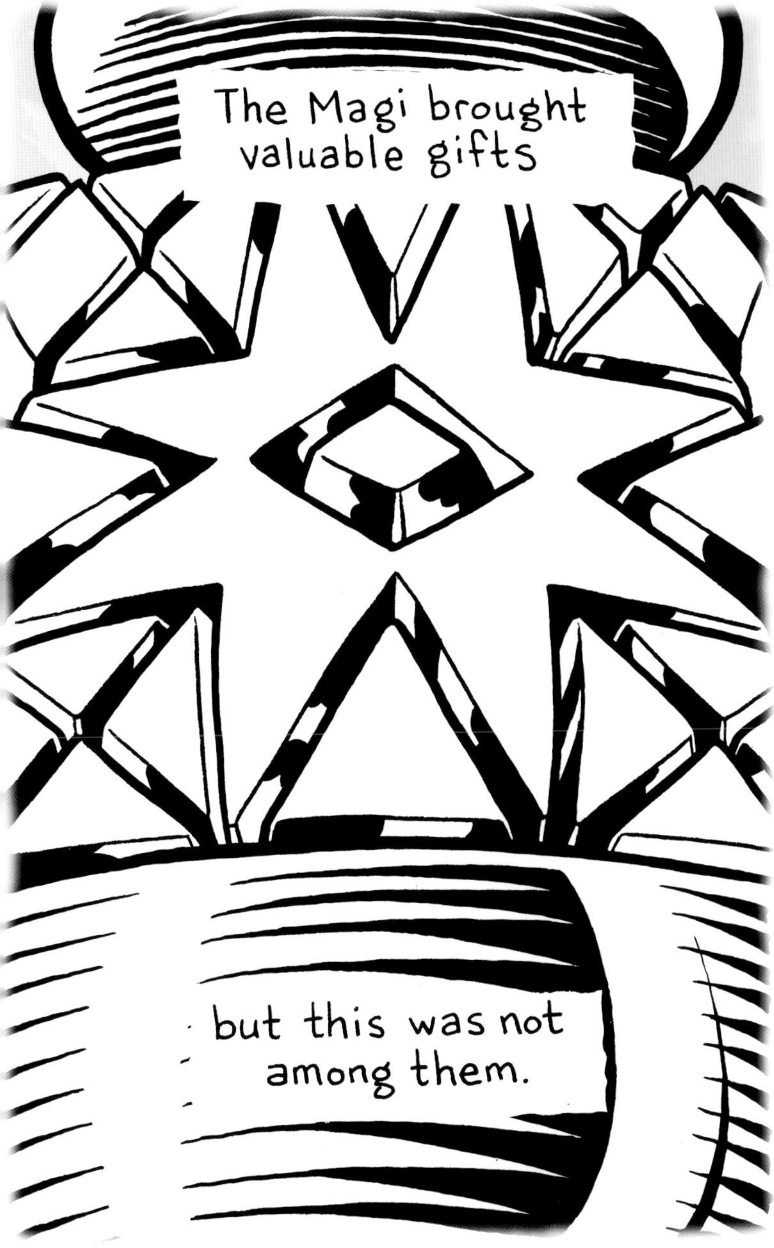
The Magi brought valuable gifts
but this was not among them.

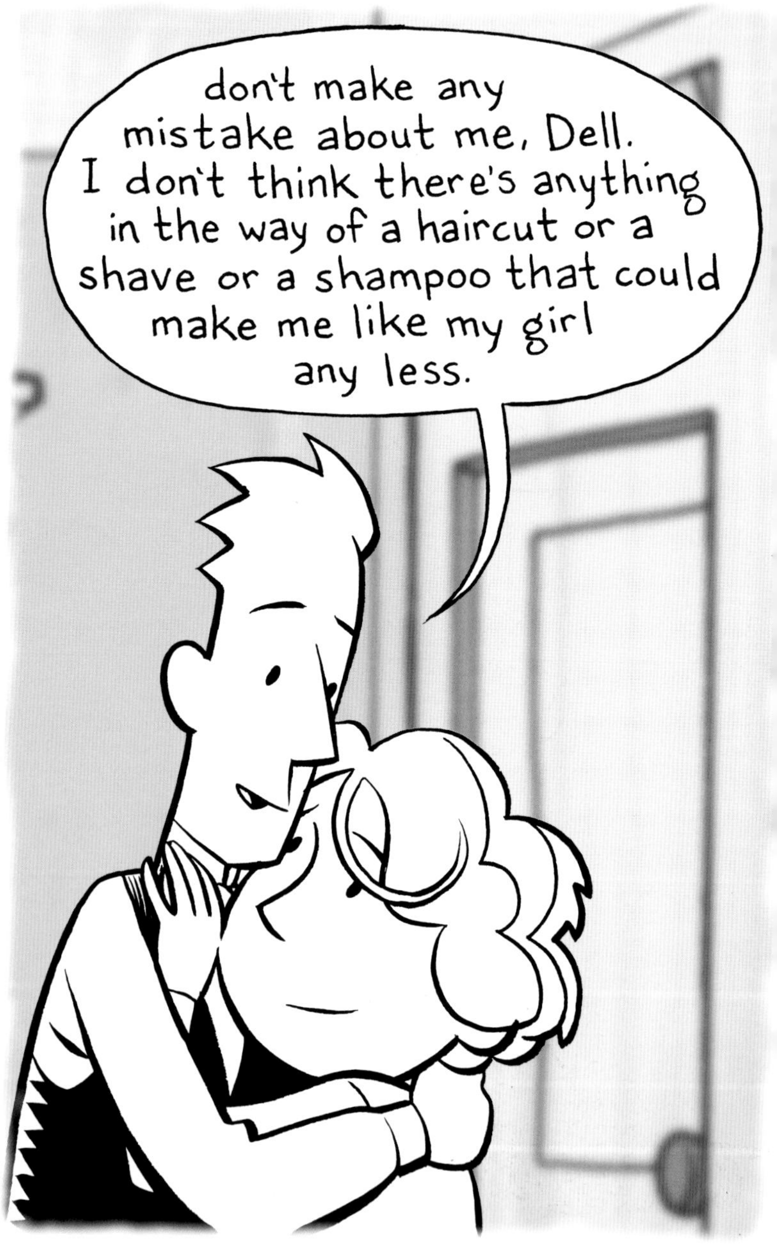
don't make any mistake about me, Dell. I don't think there's anything in the way of a haircut or a shave or a shampoo that could make me like my girl any less.

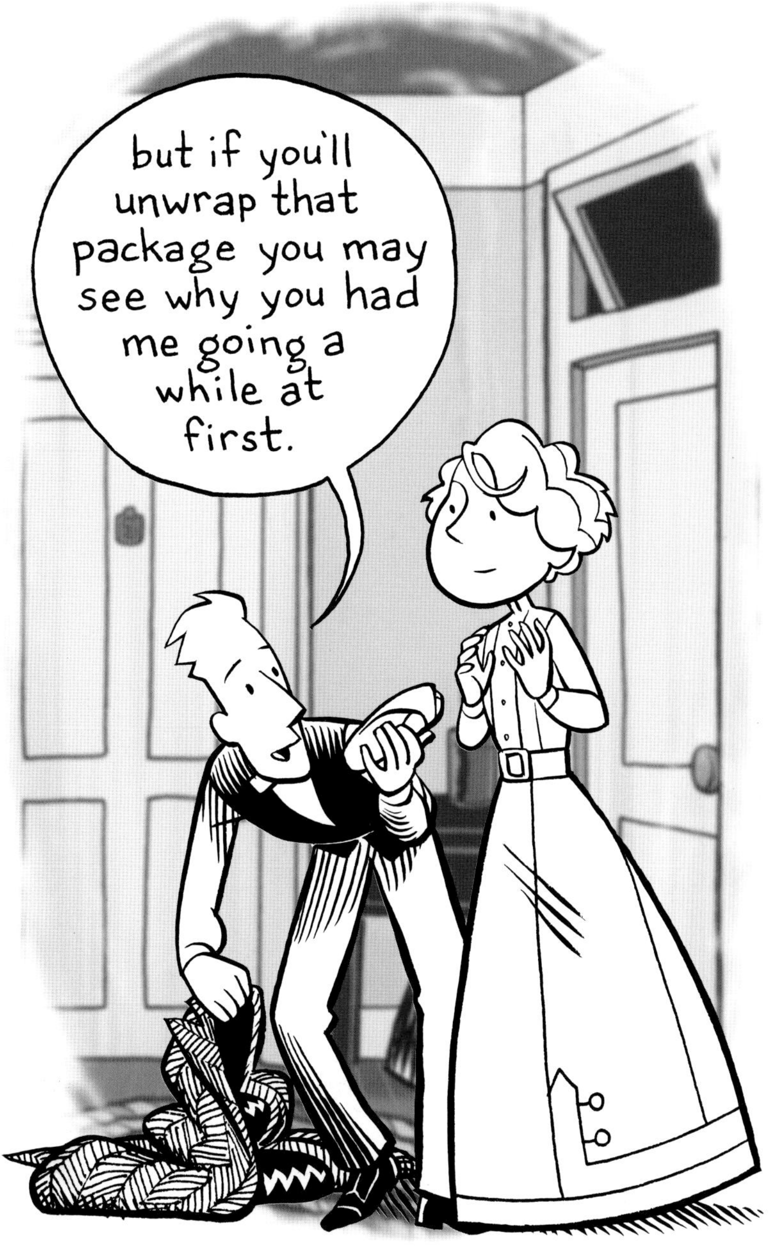
but if you'll unwrap that package you may see why you had me going a while at first.

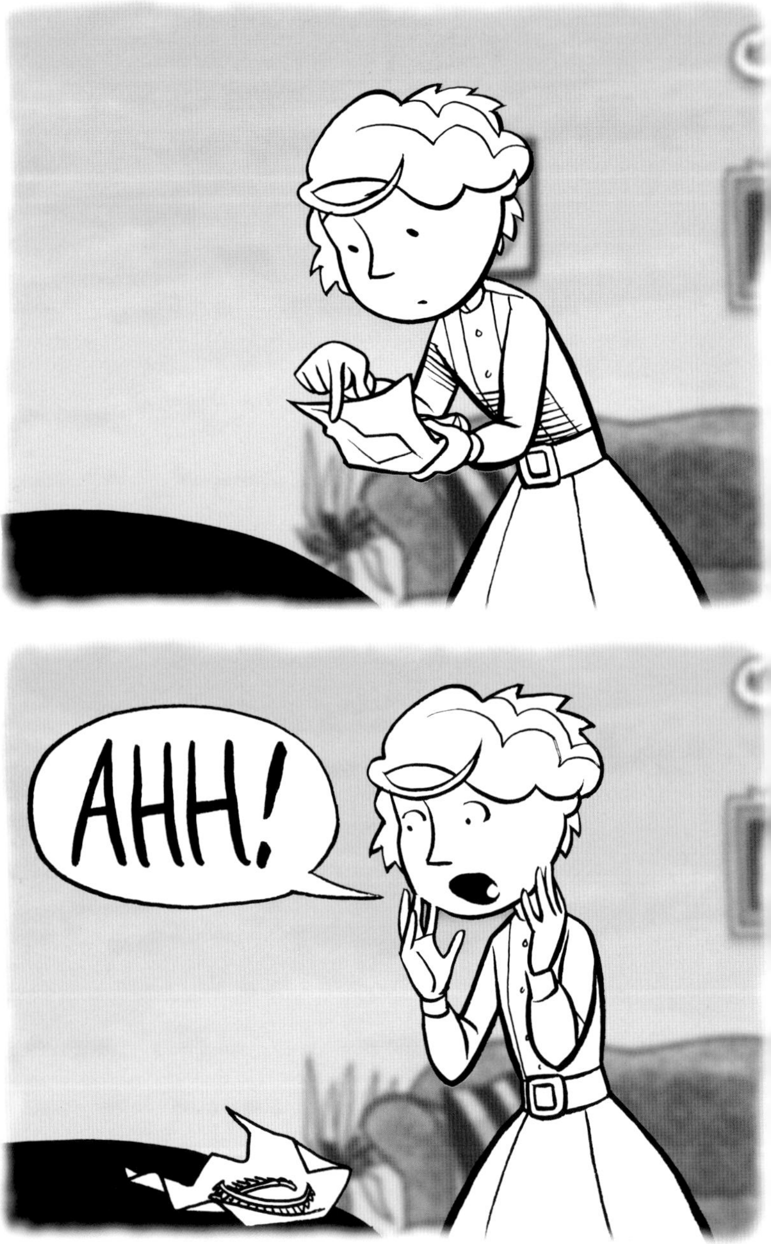
AHH!

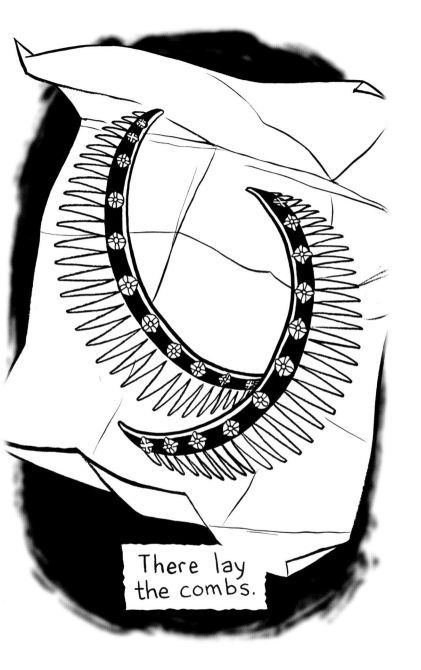

There lay
the combs.

They were expensive combs, she knew, and her heart had simply craved and yearned over them without the least hope of possession.

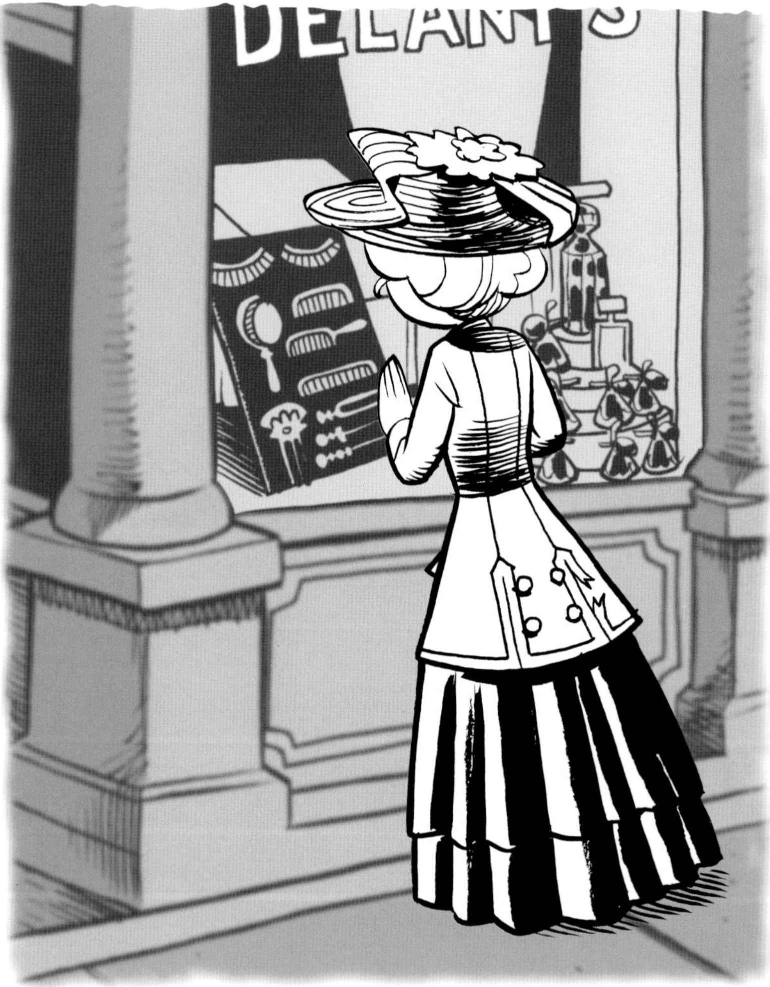

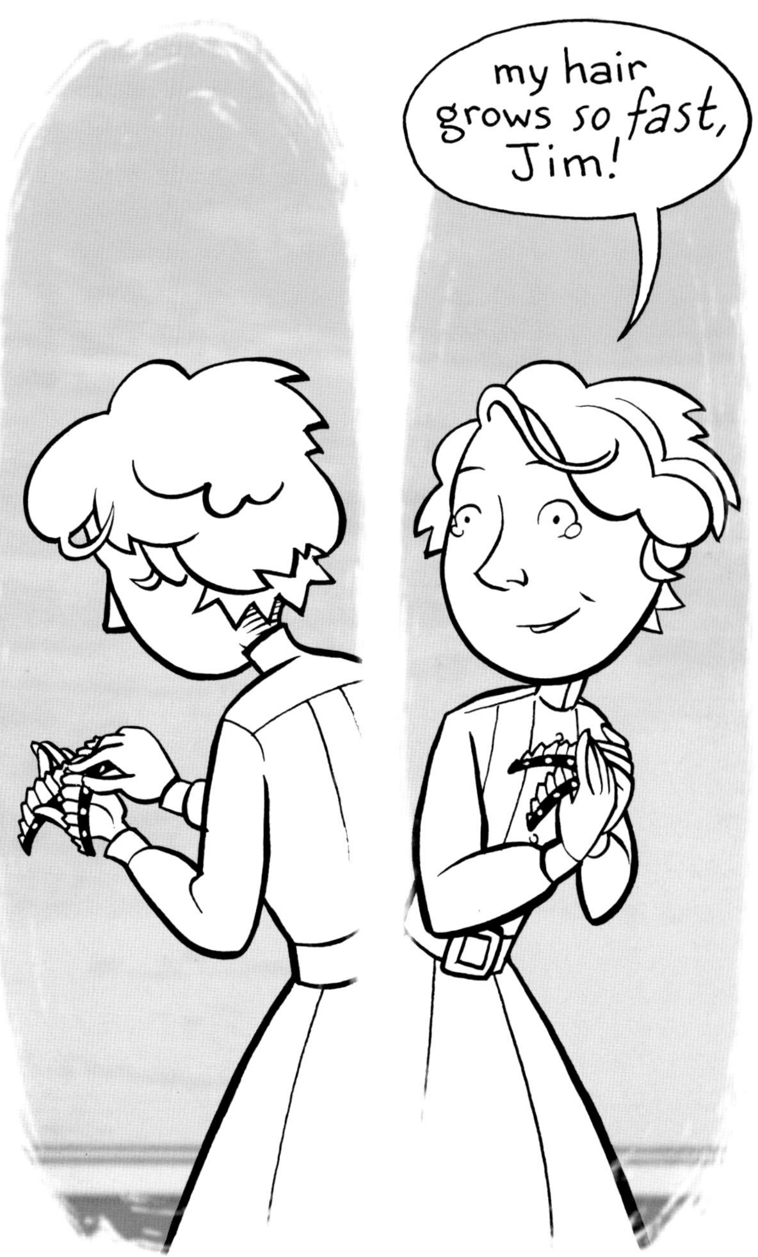
my hair grows so *fast*, Jim!

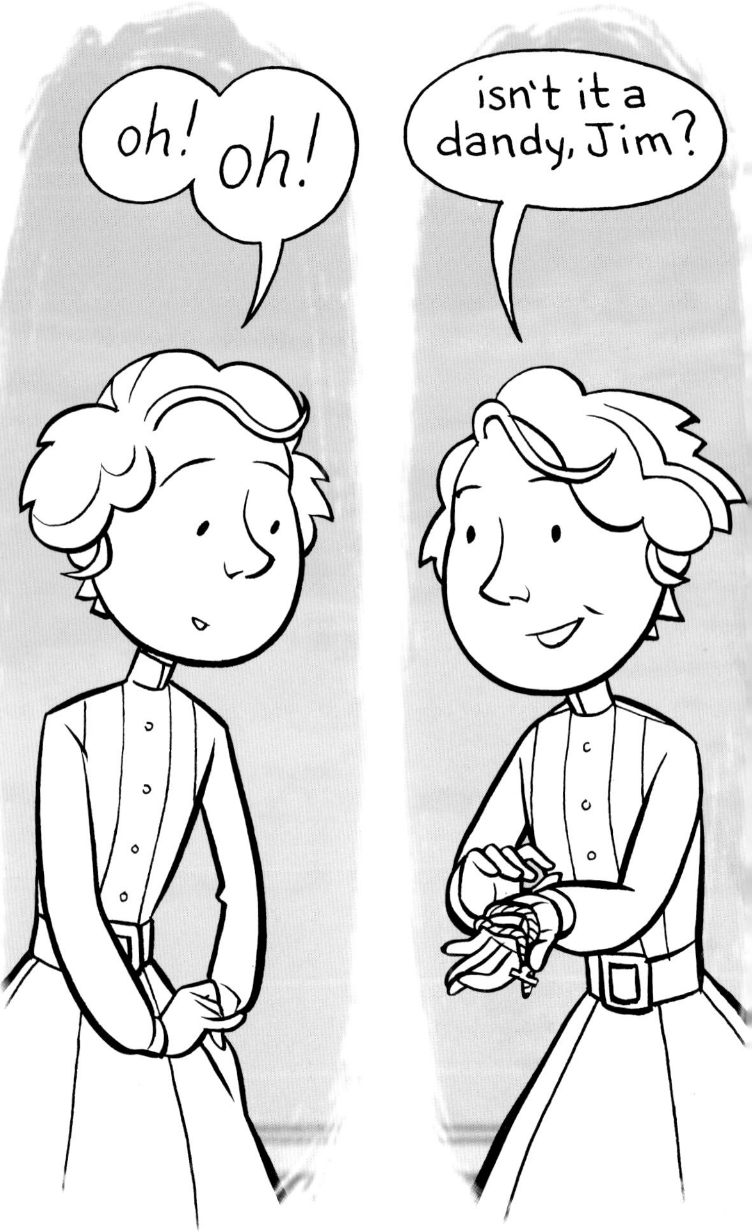
oh! oh!
isn't it a dandy, Jim?

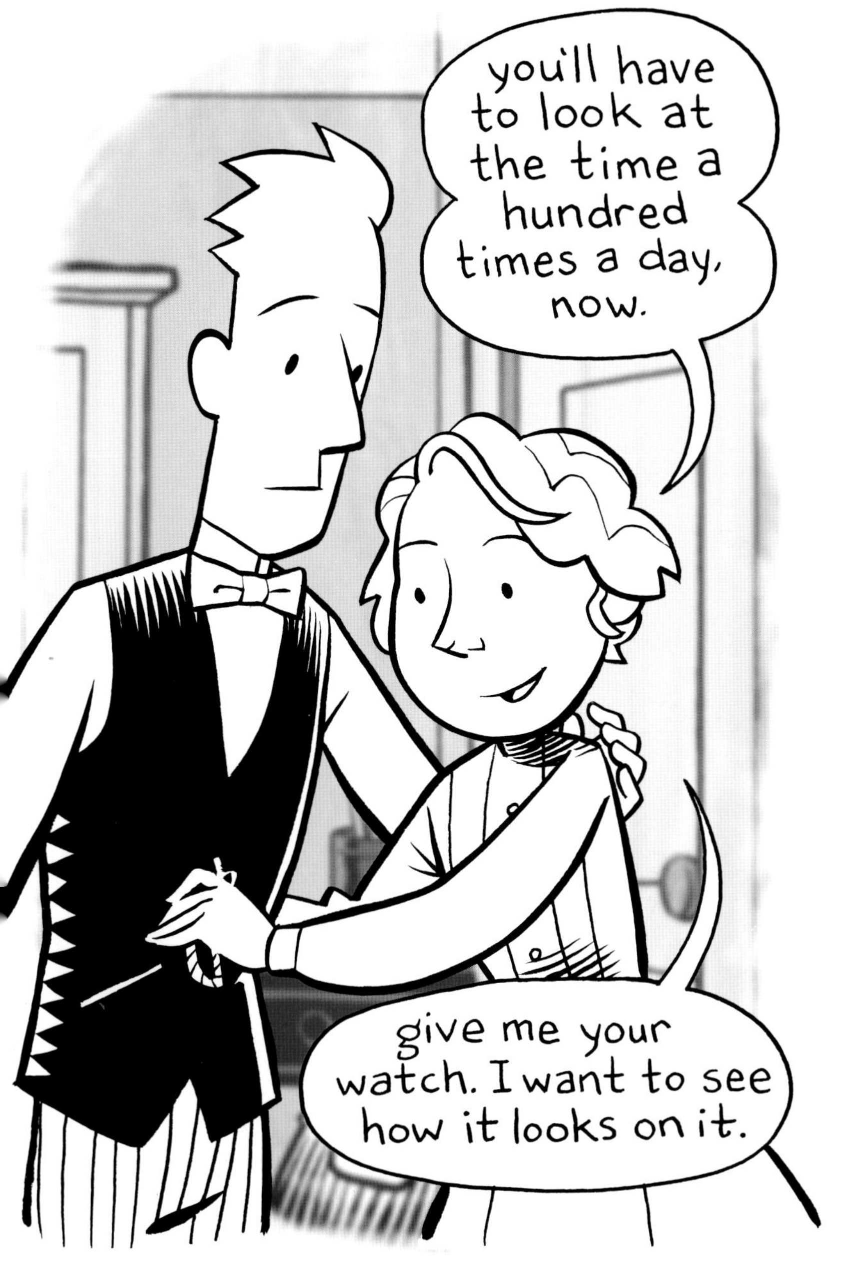
you'll have to look at the time a hundred times a day, now.
give me your watch. I want to see how it looks on it.

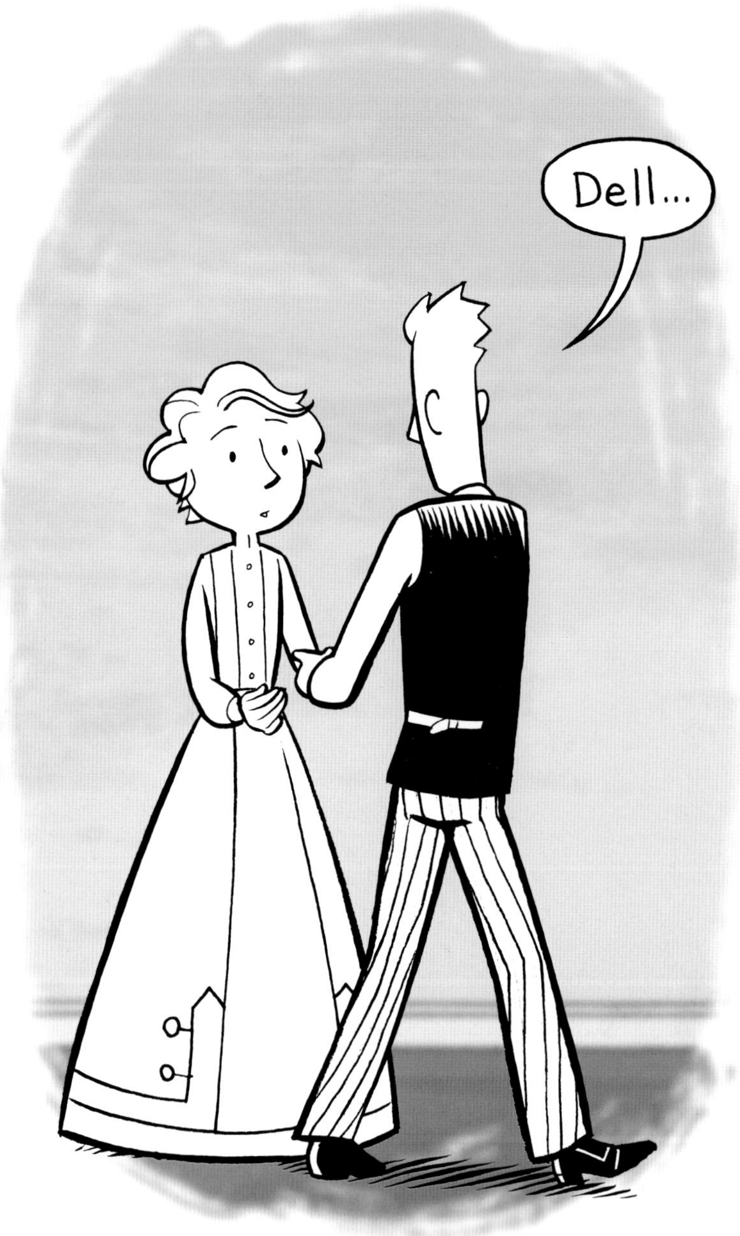
Dell...

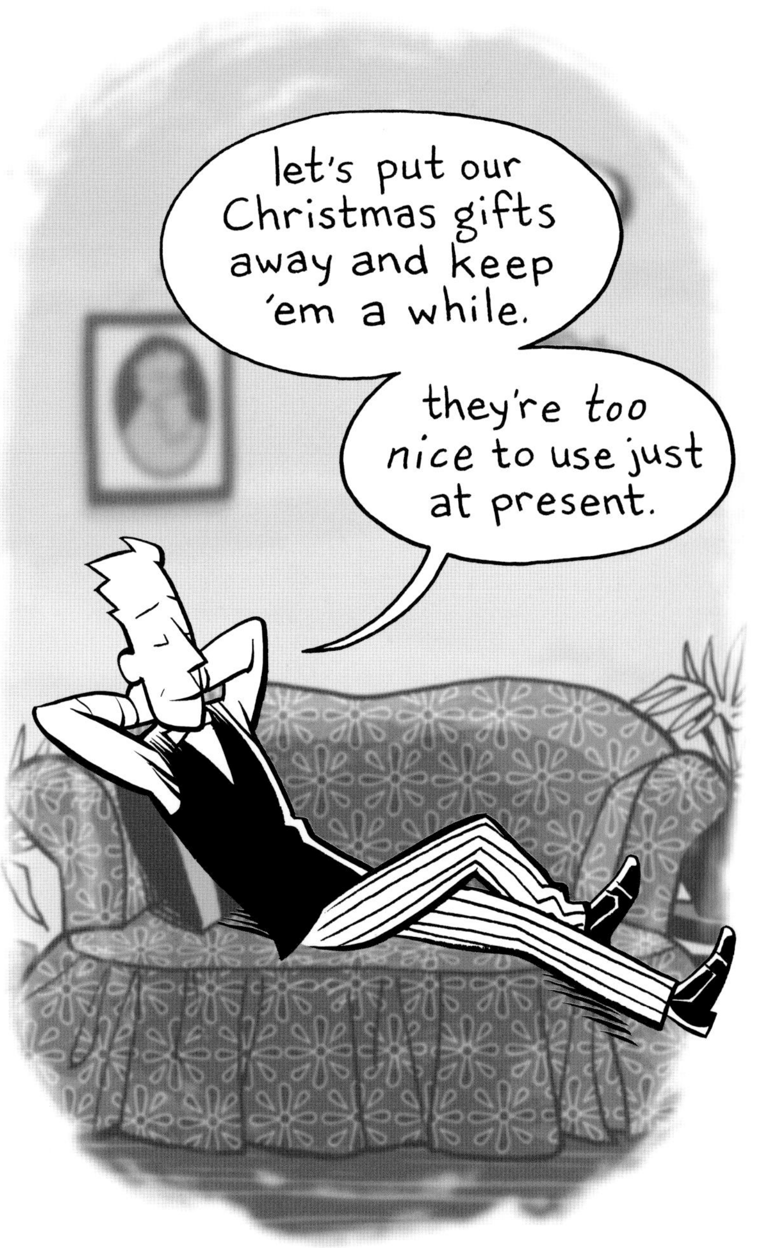
let's put our Christmas gifts away and keep 'em a while.
they're *too nice* to use just at present.

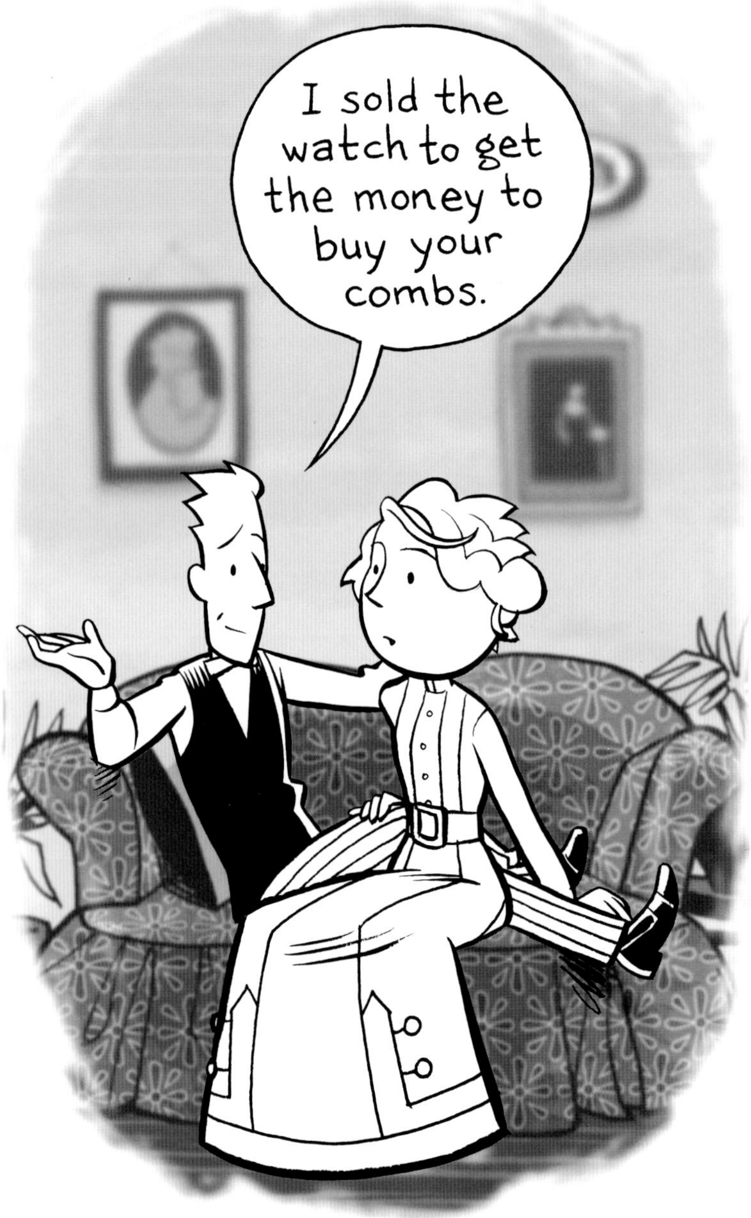
I sold the watch to get the money to buy your combs.

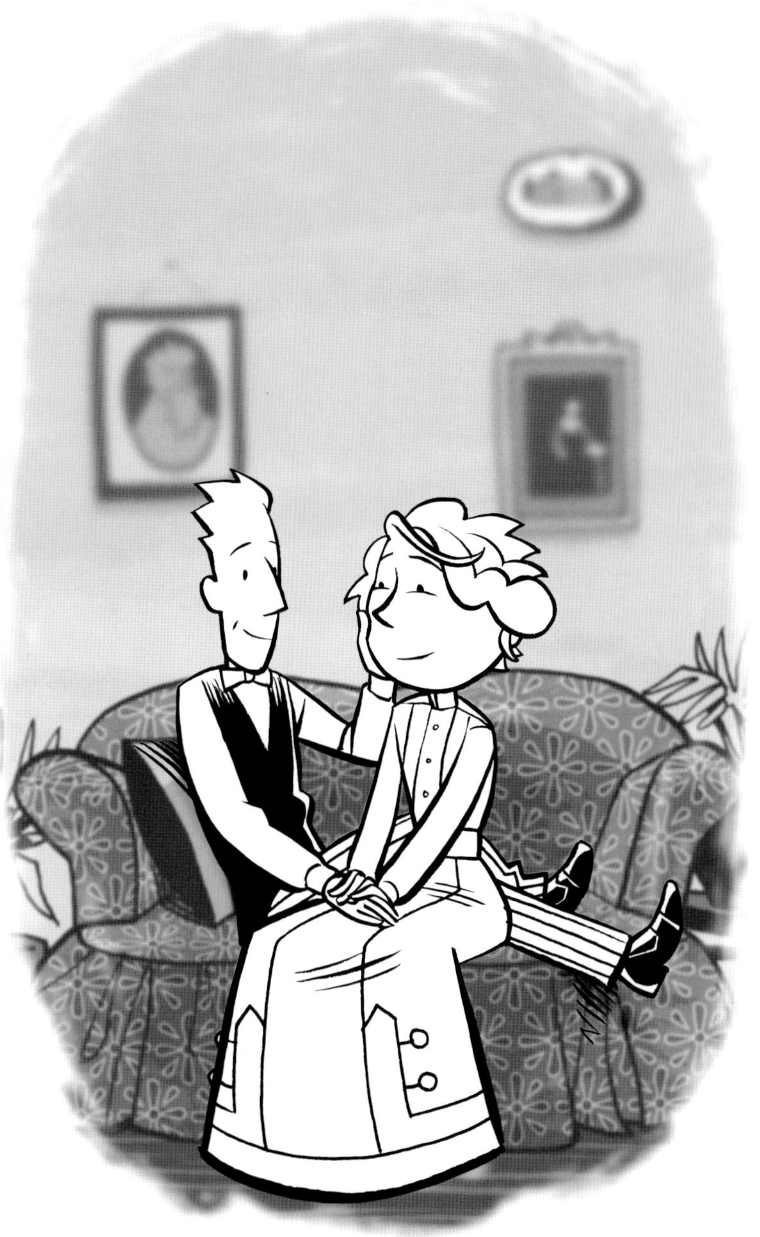

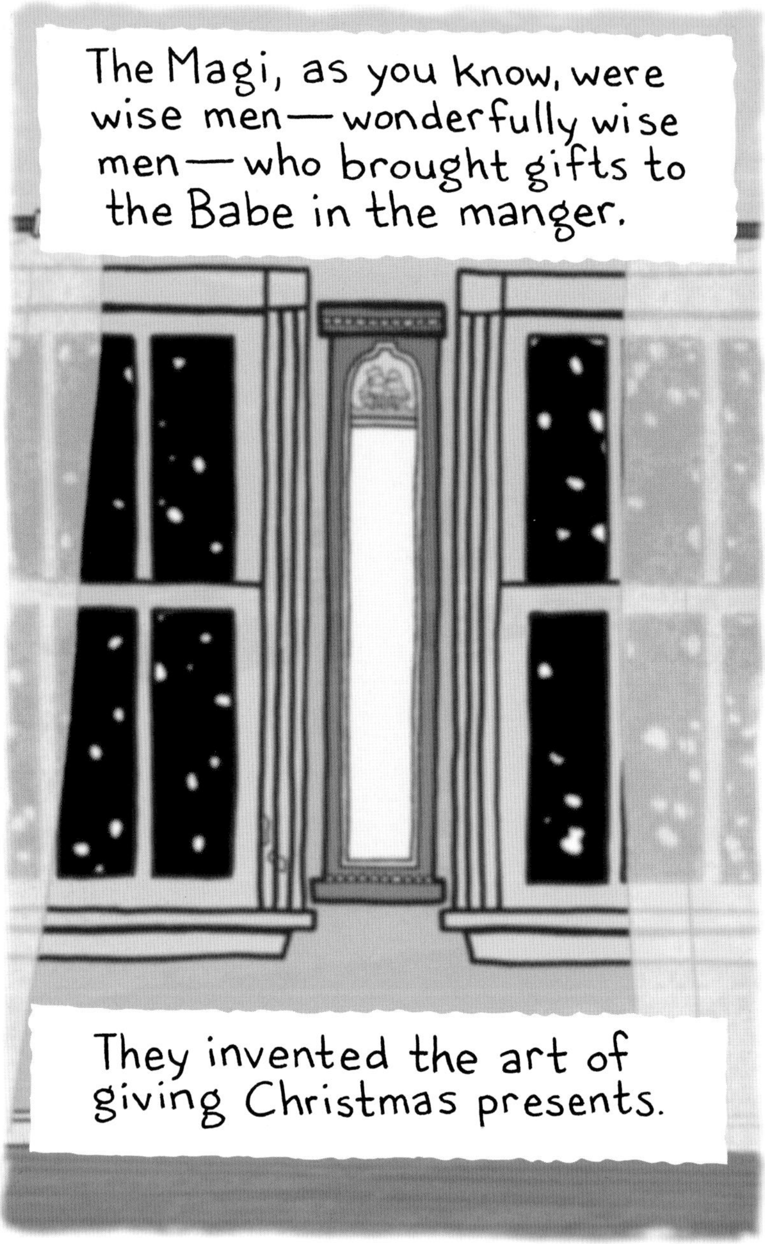
The Magi, as you know, were wise men—wonderfully wise men—who brought gifts to the Babe in the manger.
They invented the art of giving Christmas presents.

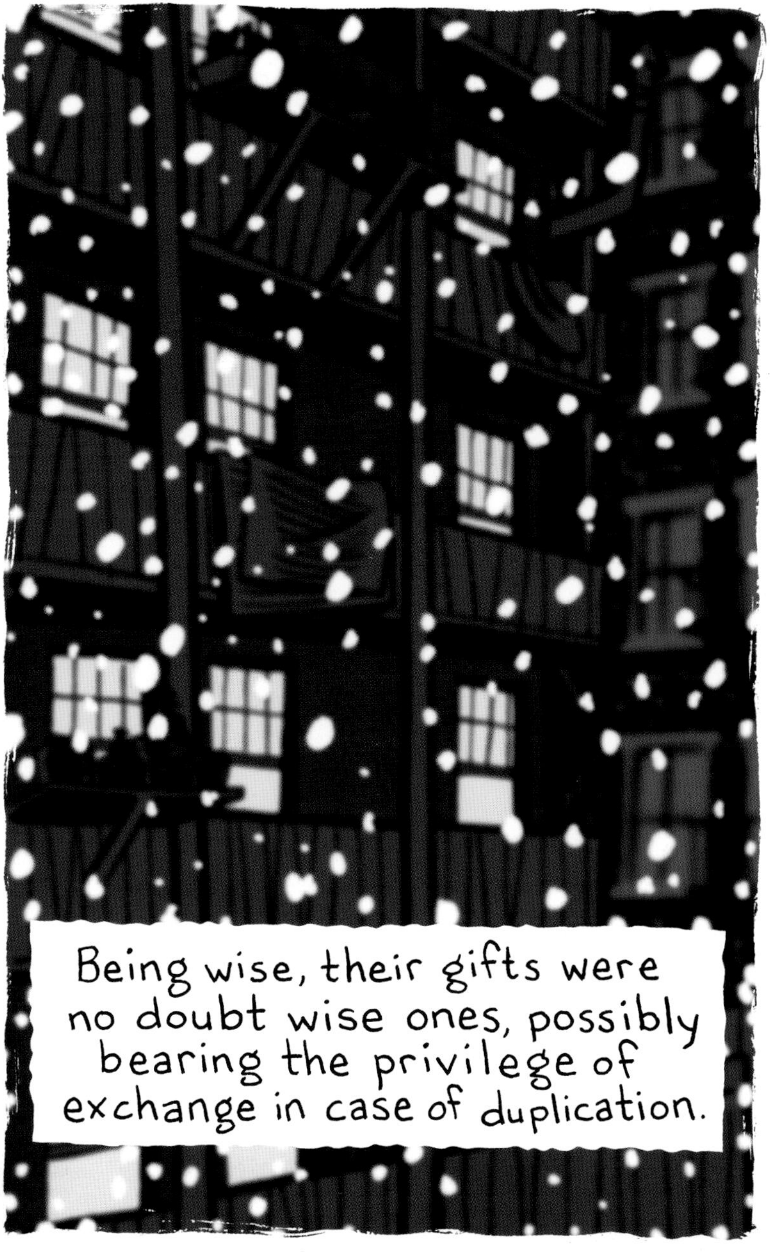
Being wise, their gifts were no doubt wise ones, possibly bearing the privilege of exchange in case of duplication.

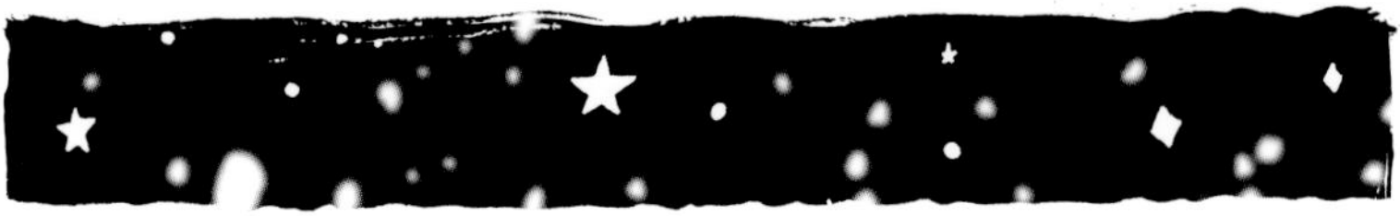

And here we have lamely related to you the uneventful chronicle of two foolish children in a flat who most unwisely sacrificed for each other the greatest treasures of their house.

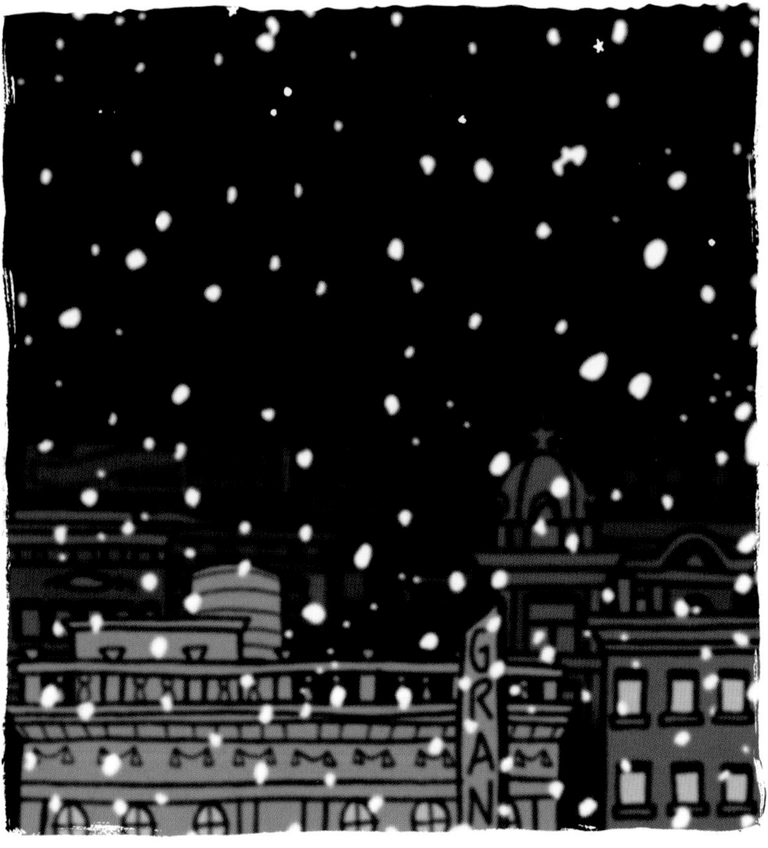
GRAN

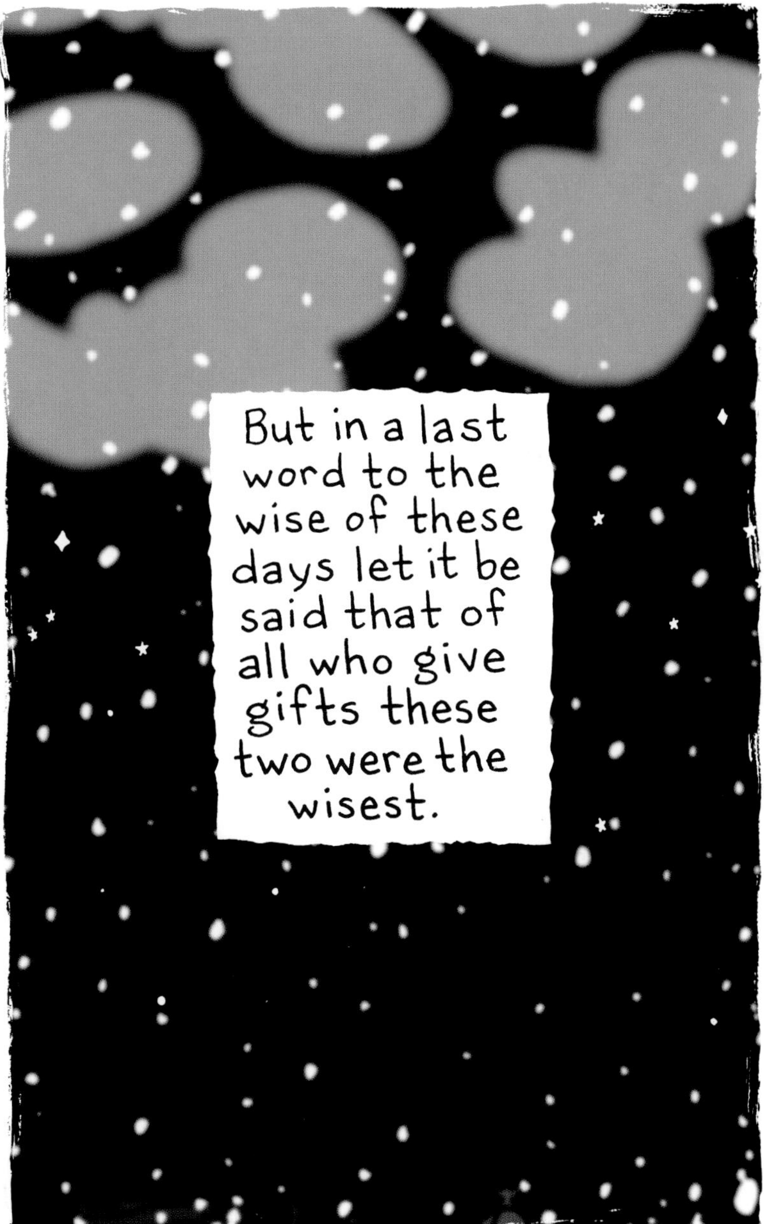
But in a last word to the wise of these days let it be said that of all who give gifts these two were the wisest.

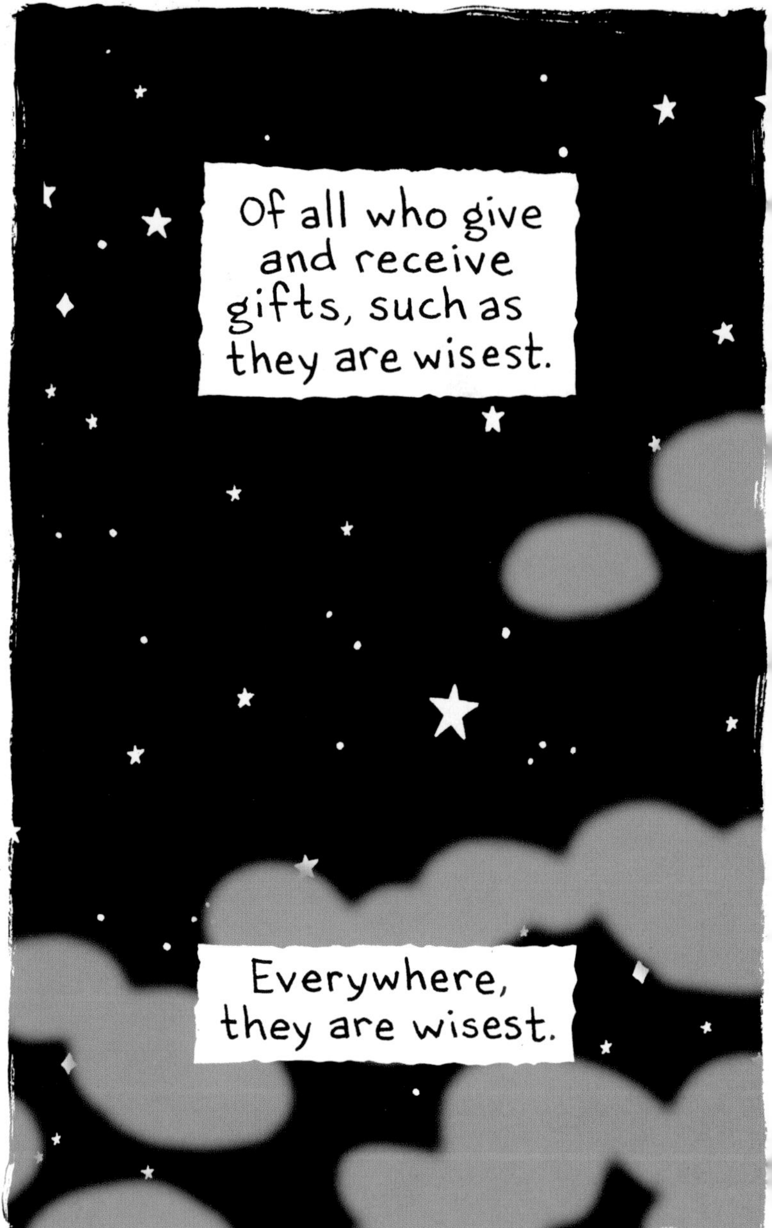
Of all who give and receive gifts, such as they are wisest.
Everywhere, they are wisest.

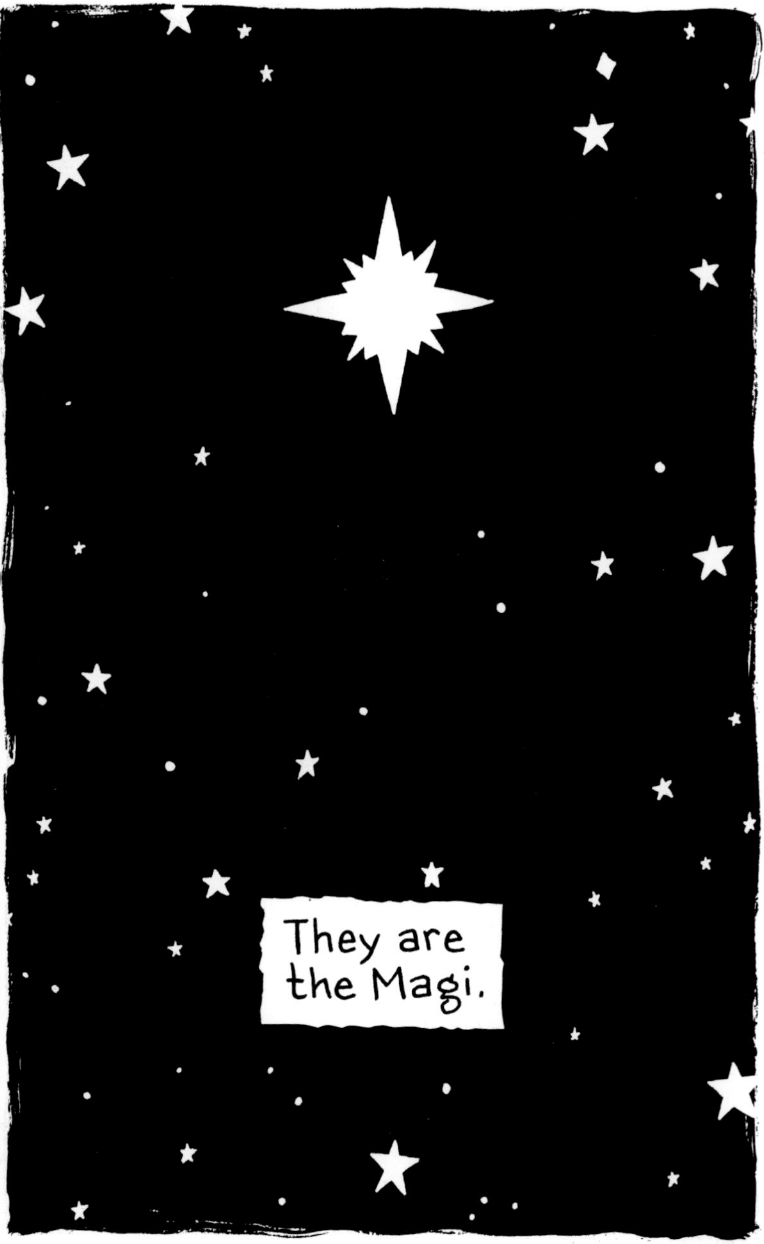
They are the Magi.